12 Step Guide For The Self-Help Book Addict

12 Step Guide For The Self-Help Book Addict

Jen Palko

Columbus, Ohio

12 Step Guide For The Self-Help Book Addict

Published by Gatekeeper Press
2167 Stringtown Rd, Suite 109
Columbus, OH 43123-2989
www.GatekeeperPress.com

Library of Congress Control Number (LCCN): 2020944511

ISBN (paperback): 9781662903922

This book is dedicated to my grandparents, Rosario and Lillian, who not only taught me to have patience in life but that any cake Grandma makes has no calories. I will forever miss bringing you both Wawa sandwiches, sitting together on your porch, and having you around in this physical world.

To anyone who has an entire bookshelf filled with self-help books and inspirational titles, it shows courage to take that first step in buying the book, a step that many don't even take. You have recognized something in your life that feels out of place and want to do better. That, in itself, requires great strength.

xo Jen

Contents

The Basis for This Book

I guess you could say that I had a calling at a young age, and I didn't even know it. I vividly remember listening to self-meditation CDs at night. During my weekends, I'd gloss through my mom's dusty old books down in the basement. Neighboring the "Sweatin' to the Oldies" VHS tapes and the "Eat This, Not That" books were Wayne Dwyer classics, Deepak Chopra's *Ageless Body, Timeless Mind* (which my mom actually had signed by Deepak himself when she saw him live probably over twenty years ago), and some other quick-fix fad diet books. I recall glancing right over Wayne and Deepak (I still have yet to read a Deepak Chopra book, and I finally caved to reading Wayne Dwyer only a couple years ago) and instead pulled a book off the shelf titled *Psychic Living*. I'd always been one to go for the less mainstream titles over the more big-hitter authors, not because I ever thought they weren't talented or insightful, but more as an attempt to appear unique. I vaguely remember picking up this hardcover at some bookstore clearance bin a number of years ago, but I never actually bothered to read it.

Only ten or so years later, I finally decided to read it. The fact that something was tugging on me to read it I took as a sign from the Universe that I HAD to because it probably held some sort of ancient code that would solve all of life's mysteries (and maybe fix some shit in my life). So I dove in. I enjoyed it. Honestly, it didn't reveal any taboo secrets that would help me take over the world or develop some serious clairvoyant abilities.

It was just an interesting read. I'll tell you what it did teach me, however. It helped me realize that even at a young age, I had been interested in things that were "off the cuff." I remember I was big into hypnosis for a little while. At the time I was making the attempt to break my emotional and binge-eating habits that I had developed when I was twenty. Honestly, I didn't even know how hypnosis worked. I was looking more for that miracle quick-fix thing overnight. I'd pop a hypnosis CD into my Discman (yes, Discman), put my headphones on, lie on my bed, and close my eyes. I think I probably fell asleep more times than I could count, and I never managed to "fix" myself like I intended. I'd start blaming myself for not having the willpower or the concentration to properly hypnotize myself. I thought I was unhypnotizable and always found myself frustrated because I thought it would be so cool having this superior power that other people didn't know about, this supernatural ability. I was bummed.

I've always enjoyed the occult—anything to do with ghosts, haunted houses, or witches. I think a lot of that was from having an older brother who collected horror movies, had exotic pets, and introduced me to death metal. I would have never known about specific characters in books and movies or my secret obsession with satanic music if not for him. He also enjoyed scaring the shit out of me on a regular basis (maybe I built some emotional resilience from that). At least a couple nights a week, he'd quietly and slowly creep across the hall that joined our bedrooms, then just as I was about to fall asleep, whisper in my ear something along the lines of, *"Jeeeennifeeeer … theeere's a witch in your wiiindow …"* or *"Jeeeennifeeerrr … Satan's coming to get yoooouuuuu."* Naturally, as an eight- or nine-year-old, I'd spring out of bed screaming, and my legs would fly (and I mean FLY) down the stairs into my mom's bedroom, where I'd jump in her bed and bury my head under the covers. Then she would yell, "GREEGG!! STOP SCARING YOUR SISTER!" I wouldn't say I have PTSD from the experience, but it has made me a little more wary when looking outside windows when it's dark. That, and I'm afraid of dark things lurking down long hallways or shadows in the corner. Even at thirty-eight, I'll still literally jump back into bed and pull the sheets up over my eyes.

Since I was introduced at such a young age, not only did that kind of thing scare me, but it intrigued me. Maybe not *as* frightening as the spidery shadow of a houseplant projected onto my bedroom wall at night, but I thought that things like hypnosis and psychic powers were of the supernatural and almost out of a science-fiction movie, something only a select few with special powers really knew how to master. I wanted to, in a sense, be able to bend reality. What I didn't realize until fifteen-plus years later was that I and everyone around me were constantly bending reality. Every. Single. Damn. Day. Bending and filtering reality. Of course, not in the literal sense because after all, no matter how hard I tried, I could never master mind-control tactics or make myself levitate like those spiritual gurus with long gray beards (I'll be honest, I never even tried). I didn't feel that enlightened, nor do I love heights.

I'd say my "spiritual journey" didn't begin until my thirties. Actually, I don't like to use the phrase "spiritual journey" very much because I feel like it scares people off, including me. It's a tad overused and sounds very woo-woo. Friends who have known me since kindergarten would probably whisper amongst themselves about how I went off the deep end, suddenly "found herself," went vegan (I haven't), and now spends her time preaching to everyone who is doing it all wrong that they need to join my super-strict religious cult and find themselves, all for a minimal fee of only $999 per month. Nah. That's not me, really. I'm still not religious, guys, no worries.

I studied and practiced acupuncture and Eastern medicine for a number of years after working in public relations and the corporate pharmaceutical world for almost ten years (basically cold calling and sitting at a desk having other people tell me what to do), and let me tell you ... I'm still not very new age. I take that back ... I mean, some of it I do like, or rather, it interests me. Yes, I use essential oils. Yes, I believe in energy medicine like Reiki and qi (I didn't use to). I even use crystals. BUT I'm not going to jump on a plane to India anytime soon (or who knows, maybe I will). I'm not going to ingest a bunch of hallucinogenic plants (it's not my style), I'm not even into yoga, and in fact, I enjoy combat sports and full-contact activities like MMA (mixed martial arts), ice hockey, and roller derby to be a ton more fun. YET, I haven't ever been able to shake the feeling that maybe there was more to life, more than just what we experience with our physical senses. I realized that, for a long time, I went through life with horse blinders on. I even went through three years of acupuncture school and several years after, not really "believing" in energy medicine and just kind of going through the motions to be different. And then one day at work, I watched ten minutes of the movie *The Secret*, and my whole world changed. (That sounds REALLY cliché, I know, but before you slam this book shut, please read on ...)

I was between treating patients at this drug and alcohol detox I worked at the time. I had been at this gig for probably four years now, offering acupuncture and essential oil therapy to patients. I remember asking one guy sitting in the back lounge what movie they were watching, and someone yelled out, "The Secret!" The movie had come out many years earlier, but they were showing it as part of their counselor's group that weekend, as Sundays were a little more laid-back for the clients. The intention was to show addicts that change is possible just by changing thoughts and self-perception. I remember one scruffy-looking middle-aged dude with a thick southern accent blurting out, "This is BULLshit maaan. I want a million dollars, but how come I don't got it?" I ignored his comment and kept watching for a few minutes before I had to take my patient's needles out in the adjacent room. I felt a fascination with the concept of being able to manifest a desire through just our thoughts and beliefs. Little did I know that those ten little minutes opened a doorway for me, and while to this day, I think *The Secret* is a little too glossy in how they describe the law of attraction on film, it changed my life in a big way. It resulted in this fascination and interest that I couldn't seem to shake, the fascination with trying to control my reality by working with the Universe, Source Energy, God, Allah, Buddha, Bob, Sarah ... whatever you want to call it. It led me down a path of years of reading, studying, meditating, and reflecting on techniques to get there, to know what other people weren't truly absorbing. It inspired me to become that supernatural superhero spiritual guru mastermind.

The basis for this book is all about choosing your reality versus it choosing you. It's about taking inspired action versus just reading about it or wishing for it all the time. We get addicted to self-help books and reading them, but they sit on our shelves never to be read again. I started "collecting" in my twenties, tons of books with exercises and meditations, and I never did ANY OF THEM ... I was too lazy and inconsistent because it all seemed too overwhelming. So I'm not going to inundate you with pages upon pages of specific exercises or meditations to implement because I, like you, wouldn't want to do them either. Instead I'm going to give you the best advice that I can give, a twelve-step guide you can refer back to whenever you want. I want you to shift your reality, but in a way that makes you expand your thinking versus repetitive exercises you won't do. My goal with this book is to make you think more about your life, what you want out of your life, and about how you're filtering your reality. By the end of it, you'll have the ability to not only shift your mindset but choose the life you want, not because I'm forcing you to do it, but because you DECIDE.

You need not "create" anything. It's more about deciding who you want to be and being that person. It's not about faking it 'til you make it, but actually embodying an ideal version of you. You don't need self-help. In fact, you don't NEED anything. You already are and already have what you think you don't have. You just need to become aligned with it in your current life.

I learned a lot as I was writing this book, actually. A few years in the making, I witnessed my own progression of thoughts and discovered new things about myself along the way, even learning new things about my goals and my reality. We are evolving human beings. We aren't designed for stagnation. We're designed to constantly evolve, learn, grow, and flow with life. That's why whenever we hit a wall, we feel uncomfortable because it prevents us from our ever-evolving nature.

Becoming an Author

I always felt in my heart that I wanted to write a book someday, or multiple books, for that matter. So I set the intention and playfully put it out into the Universe. I knew it would happen eventually, but I didn't put a time stamp on it. I didn't wait for it to happen. I didn't become frustrated that I didn't have a best seller in the local Barnes & Noble yet. I set the intention, then I let it go. I, of course, started putting the wheels in motion by actually writing stuff down, but without pressure. Just writing down my thoughts, almost like a type of therapy for myself. I set basic goals of writing ten pages a day. If I missed a session or I didn't feel like writing, I didn't question it. I never pressured myself. Instead, I played the game of "Wouldn't it be nice to be an author?" If it happened, cool. If not, then, oh well. But having it actually come to fruition was a whole lot juicier.

Writing is therapeutic in its own sense, so there is always that. From time to time, I would think about seeing a hard copy of a book with my name on the front in the local bookstore, occasionally visualizing myself at a book signing and posting about it on my social media pages and talking about it on my YouTube channel. Again, this was done playfully without pressure, in an "I know it's in me, and I know it will manifest at the proper time and place" type of way. But until then, I was going to enjoy the process and not put too much emphasis or importance on it.

For many years, I tried to force jobs, relationships, and the perfect body to appear. I wanted new opportunities to knock on my door and people in higher positions to acknowledge me when I failed to acknowledge myself. I based so much of my happiness on things externally that it became almost like a drug. I would get a taste of how amazing it felt to be acknowledged by someone badass, how awesome it felt to have someone contact me about a new job opportunity, or how excited I felt when my family would get excited for me. But I almost forgot myself in the process. I became addicted to that "feel good" rush throughout my body, and I wanted to experience that every day, not just once in a while. So I thought that if I tried repeating the process each and every time, then it would mimic that experience and those feelings. Instead, it led me down a path of the opposite effect. Why? Because I tried forcing what could not be forced. I tried forcing what was never meant to be in the first place. I tried artificially recreating the experience, but in hindsight, it wasn't the right place or the right time. I remember I'd obsessively check my emails day and night, desperately hoping someone would contact me about a new job opportunity or acknowledge my presence. I'd check my phone to see if a specific love interest texted me back. What I'd often get were crickets, or just the usual Walgreens ads for soap and blemish cream.

What was it about a job that gave me that feeling to begin with? Was it the job itself? The people? Or something else? Turns out it was more a reflection on what I lacked inside. Acceptance. Acknowledgment. Worthiness. Security. The list goes on. I think this goes for a lot of folks out there. We often think a job or money is going to cure what we lack inside, but on a larger scale, we don't need an outside source. We already possess it inside. Many times we feel like we're lacking in certain areas driven by past experiences from family, friends, or society, but we have the ability to feel accepted without relying on other people to do it for us. We have the ability to feel abundant and secure without an external job fulfilling that for us. So many times we get what we want (for example, a job), and it still doesn't fill the void. The real strategy is to look inside ourselves, discover what we truly need, and figure out ways to alleviate the void without the aid of outside sources. It involves getting to know ourselves again, which for some of us can seem completely foreign, frightening, or occasionally awesome. But the moment we can learn more about ourselves, the better off we are.

What Makes Us Listen?

It seems like everyone these days is writing a book, everyone is an "expert" at something, and everyone is trying to make a living marketing themselves or their services in some way. If everyone's always selling something, what makes us listen? What separates one person's saga from the next? The answer is connection. Once we find that we resonate with someone's story or journey, we pay attention. Once we can relate it to something we're going through and gain value from someone, we listen. How can you help someone? It can be as simple as holding the door for them or as complex as life coaching. How far you take it is up to you. There are tens of thousands of people in need every day, from that homeless person you see downtown to the woman who has recently gone through a messy divorce and is now taking care of her dying mother.

If you're like me, you're tired of Facebook sponsored ads popping up, commercials repeating themselves over and over again, waking up to spam emails you keep deleting that keep boomeranging back into your inbox, and being hounded constantly by friends and long-lost acquaintances who are always trying to sell you something. To me, the current advertising platform is extremely intrusive and very emotionally manipulative. So that's why I wrote a book to convince you that my way is the best way ever that ever was, and that my way is the only way to follow, and that everyone else is wrong, wrong, wrong. Actually, no. It's not. I disagree completely, and while some of the ideas in this book may come across as "my way or the highway," you are free to disagree. You are even free to slam this book shut and toss it out. It doesn't make a difference. I just ask that you remain open minded and listen with open ears. At least read it before you toss it out because that would be a waste of money and trees. My goal is not to persuade you to agree or disagree with me but to add any value that I can. My anticipation is that you begin to see your life and your reality as more than what you've seen all your life—to open you up to some new concepts and fun esoteric ideas. To crush the idea that life has to be hard and to refrain from bombarding you with too many to-do lists (although there might be a few ;)). I know you didn't pick up this book because you already have it all figured out. I've been a self-help addict myself, always buying and reading but never actually creating change long-term. Kind of like a fad diet. Change on the outside, but whatever is going on the inside stays put. Reverts back. I want you to change that. And you CAN change that. This book will help you do that.

Recognize your ego.
Say hello to it.

"The moment you become aware of the ego in you, it is strictly speaking no longer the ego, but just an old, conditioned mind-pattern. Ego implies unawareness. Awareness and ego cannot coexist."
—Eckhart Tolle

We've got this thing called the ego. The ego is there to protect us at all times; however, in the same token, it can also hinder our ability for change, our ability to live authentically, and our ability to live from a place of purpose. I never really thought much about the ego for the majority of my life, except for the past few years. Since then, I've paid attention to it and how much it ruled my life. I realized that every single damn day, this thing owned me.

What Planet Does the Ego Come From?

The planet where babies don't exist. That's all I'll say. No, really ... BABIES. Babies don't have egos coming out of their mother's womb. They acquire the ego from life experiences, from their parents ... then from peers, society, and other human beings. Babies slip on their ego hats once society takes hold and they become introduced to the emotions of fear and isolation. Ego essentially means "I am." It's what separates you from others and how you identify yourself. So if you start identifying yourself with a particular sector of reality, you develop an unconscious ego around it. Once you begin comparing yourself to other people, you live more out of your ego. So how do you learn to live with this thing that seemingly causes you so much harm and despair? Let's find out.

Recognize Your Ego

The first step is recognizing your ego when it's speaking. A good majority of the time, the ego isn't your voice. It's the voice of an annoying thing that has taken all of your underlying beliefs and translated it into what SEEMS like your voice. So in a sense it's you, but at the same time, it's not. It's a part of your being and your brain, but it's not the authentic version of you. The authentic version of you doesn't speak strictly out of its head; it speaks out of its heart and mind, aka the conscious and the unconscious mind.

A vast majority of people live out of their ego and don't even know it. I know for a fact that I've lived a decent portion of my life out of it because that's just what we do as human beings. It's a really difficult thing to control, to be honest, but that doesn't mean that you can't control it. The more conscious you are of the ego, the less it bothers you. Remaining present in your headspace and recognizing the differences between your ego speaking versus YOU speaking can easily shift your life. That's also a good example of how you and I can read book after book after book trying to help ourselves and still never get anywhere. It's because we aren't even conscious half the time. We're like zombie mannequins who have a little more personality, a better makeup job, and better nutritional habits.

So this is all good and fun to know, but how do you really pay attention? How, in your Night-of-the-Walking-Dead state, do you switch to being conscious? I'm sorry to say that this requires a little action on your part. You're going to have to retrain yourself to pay attention. Pay attention to your internal state, your body first, then to the things around you. Some people call this meditation or being mindful, but I call it being conscious. How many times per day does your brain keep switching back and forth between the past and the future? You're either thinking of what you did five minutes ago, what you should have done five minutes ago, what you did five years ago, OR what you're going to do five minutes, five years, five seconds from now. Where is your headspace right now, at this exact moment? Yes, you are reading these words, but in the back of your mind, can you honestly say that you weren't thinking about something else too? Were you really 100 percent focused on this book, or were you deciding what to have for lunch or dinner or recalling an experience you had from the other night? Welcome to the unconscious mind. It runs on background, and we don't even realize it until we pay attention. Then we realize … "Wow, Jen … you're right. I was just thinking of clipping my cat's toenails later," or "Wow, Jen … I really need to go to Walgreens and get more cover-up for this pimple on my forehead." See? The more you pay attention, the louder your unconscious comes to a point where you can't stop paying attention to it.

To be completely present, you must learn to first recognize the ego speaking, then retrain yourself to shut it off. "SHUT. IT. DOWN," as one of my high school cafeteria monitors, Bobby B, used to say to us all the time. Shut it down. How to shut it down? Keep reading.

Know When Your Ego is Sabotaging You

Like the Beastie Boys would say, *"Listen all y'a'll; it's an EGO SABOTAGE."* Except they never used the word "ego" in that song, did they? What exactly does sabotage mean? According to my Google dictionary, the word "sabotage" is a noun that is defined as (and this is no lie)—are you ready for it? *"Sabotage = the action of sabotaging something."* Thanks, Google. Now I can rest peacefully in my grave. I don't think that really clears it up for everyone involved, so I'll go with the verb definition instead, which is: *"deliberately destroy, damage, or obstruct (something), especially for political or military advantage."* A little better, I feel. Since we aren't talking about political or military advantage per se, I'd say ego sabotage relates more to control. Your ego is not necessarily out to destroy or damage you, but it is there to protect you from others destroying your comfort level. You and I have this ego to keep us safe from harm. To us, harm equals anything that compromises our reputation and keeps us from certain emotions that don't feel so hot and peachy. Feelings like embarrassment, shame, guilt, insecurity, fear, stupidity, unworthiness, etc. are not something we choose to live with every day. We'd prefer things like joy, bliss, excitement, and elation because these feel more like home to us.

Judgment is a good way to tell when your ego is sabotaging you, both self-judgment and judgment of other people. You judge and criticize yourself based on past programming, but also because, in a funky sort of way, confirming to yourself how you're unworthy or just an insecure person keeps you in your comfort zone. It keeps you safe. The same goes for when you judge others. You inflate your ego to the size of a Macy's

Day Parade hot-air balloon to make yourself look better than others. This again keeps you safe and in your zone. Let's say you judge someone on his or her appearance. You say, "Ohhh my gawd. That girl's hook nose is *sooooo* big and ugly. What was she thinking?" In essence, by your little critique, not only are you maintaining your dominant status over "big-nose girl," but you feel good that you're helping your brain maintain the belief that you're better than her, bragging about your dominance in the hierarchy of noses in your kingdom. That critique is really the ego, rising up to "protect" you. That way you never have to face the underlying feelings that you're actually jealous of her big nose because it would get you A LOT more attention than you're currently getting. The ego will always help us compare ourselves to other people without fault.

Own Your Ego

Don't let it own you. Your ego is not you. Really, it's not. Your ego is a PART of you, but it's not you as a whole, just like your physical body is not all you. It's a piece of your puzzle. You have your physical body, but you also have other "yous" on different dimensions. (If you don't believe me, check out the book *Living in Flow: The Science of Synchronicity and How Your Choices Shape Your World* by Sky Nelson-Isaacs, which talks about how our astral emotional body and our mental body play a part in our lives and actually cause peculiar synchronistic events.) The more you own your ego, the more you have conscious control over your reality.

So after you've recognized the ego, determined when it's speaking, and owned it, THEN what? Next is to discover how many times from your past you've made decisions based on the big E and how it's shaped you as a person. How many things in your life are because you made a decision based on your ego? Think about the career you're in, the relationship you're in, how you dress, how you act around other people, what your diet looks like, what kind of car you drive, what kind of TV shows you're into, what type of music you like, what you do for fun, etcetera, etcetera, etcetera ... For example, what made you decide to go into the profession you're in? Did you start listening to a particular type of music based on other people's recommendations or the media? Or did you decide as a baby that you really enjoyed gangsta rap? Do you wear skinny jeans with holes in them, and is that REALLY your style, or do you find it extremely uncomfortable and always find yourself trying to pick out wedgies? Think long and hard about this. If you made every ounce of your decisions based on just you and not other people, places, and things influencing you, you'd probably consider yourself pretty damn different or make completely different choices in your life. Do you read certain self-help books because they were suggested by someone else or they sit out on the center aisle of your local Barnes & Noble on clearance? (Hopefully, not this one ... at least not yet). Now you can see how extremely difficult it is to pinpoint whether we've made our decisions based on influencers in our environment or based on US. We're exposed and vulnerable to take in everything with our senses. That's called being human, so there's no way to fight it, really. The best we can do is pay more attention to what or who is influencing us and our decisions in life.

Your Ego and Creating Change

First of all, I don't like to use the word change, so I'm not so sure why I just used it. I like the word "shift" much better. It just sounds better, don't you think? SHIFT. It's just one of those words that gets you. It creates some sort of emotion that makes you feel kind of giddy. Change sounds boring, and to me, the word implies that we aren't good where we are. We lack something outside of ourselves, but SHIFT sounds like we're actually versioning ourselves up to a higher level. An upgrade. Yes, I like it. In essence, I believe you don't need to change a damn thing about yourself. You are already whole and complete, but you could use an upgrade in your reality and a higher version of you that already exists. You see the difference in how that sounds? Now this is important stuff ... how we talk about ourselves and the words we choose make a HUGE difference, but we'll get to that later on. For now, we're still going to focus on your ego and how it's shaped you.

If you can get to a point where you can retrain yourself to stop always listening to your ego, you will be able to shift your life. The thing with most self-help books is that they teach you the methods for change in your life, but most people haven't learned to drop their ego first to lay the foundation for shift-work. If you want a great recommendation that delves deeper into the ego, Eckart Tolle's *The Power of Now* is the book for you (although you may have read it already because it's a popular one).

Attachment and the Ego

Now that we've clarified what the ego is and what it does, let's talk about something near and dear to us all: ATTACHMENT. And no, I don't mean attachment like the static cling on your sweater or the piece of plastic wrap that keeps sticking to your hand, or even your boyfriend back in sixth grade. What I'm talking about is YOUR attachment to people, places, and things, NOT their attachment to you. We attach to specific things in life including money, status, career, relationships, material possessions, food, and health, but often our constant attachment creates an imbalance within us. This imbalance is created because we've put something or someone so far out of reach or up on a pedestal. We idolize a celebrity, for example, or we attach to food for comfort. We attach to money by placing excessive amounts of importance and appeal on it. In turn, we often create an environment where it's difficult to actually obtain the very thing we want because we've placed it so far out of reach. By creating this separation (e.g., I am here, and you are over there), we create a mismatch and never actually align with it.

This, my friend, is attachment to the ego. Ego = separation of self from the outer world; therefore, whenever we're attaching to things outside (money, cars, houses, relationships), we're also attaching to the ego and its false sense of self.

We're all made of the same stuff.

*"Since every potential in the universe is a wave
of probability that has an electromagnetic field
and is energetic in nature, it makes sense that
our thoughts and feelings are no exception."*
—Dr Joe Dispenza

Once you've been formally introduced to your ego, you can start expanding your thinking and discover that you aren't the only person going through something. And I know we often feel that way when life takes hold of us. We feel isolated, like no one understands or is going to understand, and that we're a lost cause. If you didn't feel that way, you wouldn't be seeking out books to help you grasp an understanding of your life. However, realize that the moment you cut yourself off from others, which, by the way, is totally an ego thing, you ruin your chances of winning the game we call life. At the end of the day, we're all made of the same stuff. Atoms. Molecules. Energy particles. Dense matter. Source energy. Electricity juice, stardust. Whatever name you choose to label it, we're all the same stuff.

Energy is like the Charlotte's web of electromagnetic vibrational frequencies (say that ten times fast). It connects everything in the Universe: atoms and particles. And all atoms and particles vibrate at a particular frequency, so everything we see as solid isn't actually solid. It's only solid to our senses, but in actuality, it's vibrating. We all have an electromagnetic energy field around our bodies where we can give off and receive energy from other people, places, and things. This is why lower emotions like hatred and anger can become contagious, but I'll get into more of that later. Rather than me try to explain it in too much detail, I'll quote one of my favorite authors, Penney Peirce, here:

> *You are surrounded by many energy vibrations in the outside world, from the eighty-one octaves of electromagnetic frequencies, to the vibrations of sound and heat, to the earth's Schumann Resonance, to the basic wavicles of matter. Some are perceptible through your senses, but most are not. In your inner world, you're alive with vibrating waves of energy and consciousness, from the cycles of your breath and heartbeat to your electrical brain waves. Within your brain wave levels are a variety of awarenesses, from the seven kinds of chakric consciousness to awareness of after-death experiences and other dimensions ...*

> *Your personal vibration or energy state is a blend of the contracted or expanded frequencies of your body, emotions, and thought at any given moment. The more you allow your soul to shine through you, the higher your personal vibration will be. Your personal vibration is affected by other people's vibration and the*

vibrations of the world, yet ultimately, how you want to feel is your choice.[1]

In summary, our bodies vibrate at a certain frequency and try to match up with other frequencies. Think of it like a game of checkers. Let's pretend for a minute that the red checker pieces represent a high frequency and the black checker pieces a low frequency. If we're the red checker pieces, we're always going to try to match up with other red checker pieces (similar energy and vibration). Whenever we match up with our like-minded pieces, we're also magnifying our intensity, thus growing in strength. We then have the choice to either freely move away from our black low-frequency counterparts or simply overpower them.

Remember Who You Are

At the end of the day, we need to remind ourselves that we're all the same. That beautiful actress who makes millions of dollars per year and has a rich, handsome, famous celebrity husband, a white picket fence surrounding each of her six mansions on the beach, drives one of her BMWs, Mercedes, or Range Rovers (depending on which day of the week), has perfect skin, perfect hair, the perfect Barbie body, and the perfect amount of confidence to boot? She poops too. She wakes up certain days, her hair a tousled, knotted mess, and looks in the mirror only to discover the biggest, ugliest, reddest, honkin' pus-filled pimple on the tip of her nose, and you know what she does? She

---

[1] Peirce, Penney, *Frequency: The Power of Personal Vibration* (Hillsboro, OR: Beyond Words Publishing, Inc., 2009): 49.

cries. She cries because she's got a really big in-person interview with a really big movie CEO guy later that afternoon, and she knows she can't airbrush real life. She feels insecure like the rest of us. She is a living, breathing, pooping human being, so don't believe all you see on television or on the cover of Star magazine. We're all the same "stuff" on a molecular level. If you were to dissect and dissolve us down to our very origin, the atom, you would see that everything originated from one single point of energy. What comes afterward is just a reflection of that energy being pieced together like a magnet. So never believe that you and I are different. We may appear that way on our outer shell, but this is just our brains projecting the image.

Accepting Our True Source

For as long as I can remember, I always wanted to feel accepted. As a child I'd constantly nag my father, "Look at me! Look at me! Photograph ME! Film ME!" (My dad happened to be an avid family photographer and videographer). In fact, I don't remember a lot from my childhood other than what was on those old VHS tapes or in photographs (which was a lot actually). I had a relatively normal upbringing. I had parents who provided for me, spoiled me and my brother occasionally, grandparents who adored us, and cousins and friends we'd see on a regular basis. I'd say my teenage years into my twenties were probably the most difficult. I feel like this is the first time where one struggles with self-acceptance to a greater degree. This is the time where everyone faces massive shifts in their life … the jump from elementary school to high school. Drama escalates to a whole new level and suddenly we are "adults." Then comes the start of college (at least for me), often a throwback to being a kid again. We go out with friends, we party, and we forget that we're in school to work and learn. These are the turning points in people's lives: times of transition. I'm sure you can think of a few-too-many times you did something irresponsible. We learn. We grow. We rediscover ourselves on a whole new level in our thirties or forties (depending how old you might be), as opposed to our pre-teens, our teens, and even our twenties. What's the difference? Coming back to our source. We've tried things and they didn't work out, we did what we thought was expected of us, we got the high school diploma, then maybe the college degree, the stable job with decent benefits, AND the husband (or wife) and kids, yet we still feel like we've lost part of ourselves. Maybe it's the discovery that all of the superficial stuff looks good on paper but doesn't seem to make us happy after all. We start to lose sight of who we once were and what once made us happy in life. We realize that what we've been searching for has always been inside us, our true source, yet we were too oblivious to see it.

What exactly is our true source? We keep talking about it, but what exactly is it and how do we get back to it? True source is not as complex as it might sound. It's not some psychic woo-woo magic either. True source is just what is. It's who we REALLY are ... like deep down ... deep, deep, DEEP down. It's what we're left with when we peel back all the superficial layers of ourselves. It's essentially energy, or consciousness, or awareness ... whatever you'd like to call it. It's our being broken down into the tiniest components until we're left with just energy in its purest form, connecting us to everything and everyone around us. This is the Dao or the infinite or God or whatever. We're made of the same stuff as the trees, our pets, our parents, the grass outside, and the chair we sit on at work. It can be difficult to wrap our heads around, but it's those times of change, those times where we feel unhappy, discontent, or stuck, when we begin thinking of the bigger picture, which ironically usually brings us back to a place of simplicity. Suddenly, we find ourselves wanting to find meaning and purpose in all that we do. In reality, there's no searching required. There is only breathing, letting go, and being open to the universal love inside us all. Love is more than a bunch of scruffy-looking Grateful Dead fans standing in a circle with their hands interlocked; it's our true state of being.

We Can Use Our Vibration to Shift Our Life

We all have the capability to shift our vibration. Ever hear the term "high vibe"? Well, it's for a reason. When you're in a "high vibe" state, you're feeling good, like really good. Or you might tell someone about how you've been feeling so "low vibe"; in other words, not feeling so great. You see how this works? Physics is easy if you want it to be! Seriously though, these terms were coined for good reason because we all have an innate ability to shift into a higher vibrational state versus a lower one. It's not rocket science, but we forget what it actually means sometimes. We just toss it around like a hot potato without really thinking about it.

Synchronicity and Symbols from the Universe

Contrary to what the media or your parents lead you to believe, the world is not out to get you. It's a loving place, and it wants you to succeed. The Universe is not conspiring against you, nor does it want to see you suffer. Your suffering and hardships in this world are a reflection of your own beliefs (an illusion). If you don't believe that life is hard, it won't be for you. If you constantly think of yourself as unlucky in love, in life, and in relationships and that you walk around with a black cloud hovering exactly ten feet above your head at all times, the world will provide you with more dark clouds.

We have spiritual guides on our side at all times. These are groups or individuals of a higher power in a different dimension that we know very little about. Sound a bit kooky? A little too sci-fi? Maybe so. I thought the same thing. These are things or beings that we cannot understand or comprehend in our linear three-dimensional brains. There are things about our lives, things going on behind the curtains, that we never pick up on a conscious level. The more we can tune into our subconscious selves and the more we can feel source energy circulating throughout our bodies, the more we can tap into these higher dimensions for optimal states of peace and self-growth.

Each one of us has the ability to tap into a higher self, a higher dimension. Some of us are more intuitive than others, but each of us has psychic potential. The fact is that most of us are too distracted to ever tap into it fully. We get glimpses here and there, but we often put a deaf ear to it. This is where our spiritual guides come in. The Universe and our guides provide us with clues and red flags all the time. So what do these signs look like? A gut feeling, a symbol, a soft whisper in our ear, something seen out of the corner of our eye, or a warming or cooling sensation. We are literally hit with indications all the time, guiding us along our path. The secret is training ourselves to listen, pay attention, and feel these higher dimensions.

It's like facial recognition. Imagine how many different faces of different strangers you see in a day. How about a week? A month? A year? If you had to estimate, it would equal a helluva lot, right? Now, think about how many of those faces you actually remember. I'm just taking a wild guess here, but probably less than 75 percent. The only reason you'd tend to remember a face is if your brain developed some sort of relationship or association with this person. You may see someone who works at the nearby supermarket as a cashier, and after seeing them two times or more, you'd now probably recognize them every time you went in to buy your Fruit Loops. Or say you see someone only once in your life ... a good-looking, muscular guy with lovely baby-blue eyes, long blonde flowing hair, who slightly resembles Fabio as he's ringing up your fake butter, who makes eye contact with you and is "extra" friendly with you, making funny conversation about cheese and olives. Suddenly, you can't help yourself from thinking about this Fabio doppelgänger and the way he scanned your butter across the counter. That beautifully structured jaw line is imprinted in your mind. Why? Because you had a memorable experience with him that day in the local ShopRite. You struck up a conversation with him, thereby developing a relationship/association in your brain. Now every time you think of that particular ShopRite, you think of that guy's muscles, his baby-blue eyes, and butter. You put less importance on what to buy for dinner, and your association creates a feeling of excitement and bliss throughout your body.

Now, let's say you go to that same grocery store the following week, anticipating your secret love affair through eye-contact-flirtation methods with fake Fabio, but you're very disappointed to discover that he isn't working that day. You're super bummed. You still go about your time picking up the usual staples, then solemnly walk over to the checkout line. The cashier rings you up, but you're distracted. You're fumbling around with the *Woman's World* and *People* magazines on the shelf, eyeing up all the chocolate you'd like to inhale right now. The cashier hands you your change, you each mutter the usual "thank yous" as appropriate, then you leave. You may have glanced up at the cashier once or twice, but chances are you'd have forgotten his face after a couple days. There was no true connection or conversation happening out of the ordinary. This guy wasn't nearly as noteworthy, not to mention you were distracted.

It's the same with connecting to your higher self. The more present and aware you are, the more you'll notice the smallest details, symbols, and synchronicities. The more you notice, the more tapped in you are to the higher parts of yourself, your guides, and the Universe at large.

Perspective and Perception

What you think, you create. You've heard this phrase more than once, I'm sure. In order to recognize our spiritual guides and the higher parts of ourselves, we first need to shift our perception. Our perception plays a large role in our ability to manifest physical things into our lives. Manifesting starts from the inside out. It all starts with us and how we perceive ourselves in our world. If we go about our lives and consider everything to be shit, then shit it will be.

To change our perception of the world, we must first change our perception of how we see ourselves in the world. We can't view the world around us as beautiful and loving if we hate ourselves. We can't view the world as a peaceful place if we don't have peace within ourselves. The world around us shifts as we upgrade to a greater sense of inner calm. Yes, this requires some patience, but if you can master the art of truly knowing and loving yourself, situations around you will drastically change for the better. How do we shift our perceptions? This goes back to those subconscious beliefs we hold onto. For example, if we've been taught to believe that we aren't worthy of what's good in this world, then we need to take the time to shift that mindset. It starts with exploring those beliefs in the first place. How are you currently seeing yourself in the world? What do you feel holds you back the most? Where do you feel the most out of balance? Could it stem from a past situation where you felt similar emotions? Did you ever feel abandoned when you were younger? Understand that beliefs can become "stuck" in our brains, almost like a really bad '80s song that's stuck on repeat in your head. The only way to get rid of it is to lower the volume or switch tracks.

Focus on Self-acceptance First

If we don't accept ourselves, how are we supposed to convince ourselves that we are worthy of good things or that we can change? We can't on a deeper level. How do we learn to accept ourselves? By getting in alignment with our true being, our source energy. Oh, and giving ourselves permission to do so.

By feeling in our bodies, we find out what drives us and brings us joy without the influence of other people. This requires a little work, a little soul searching, but it need not be a painful process. It's about breaking out of the same routines, the same people, places, and things. Focus on your strengths first. Are you a caring person? Do you feel good when you help other people? If so, why? What about it makes you feel good? Are you a good listener? What parts about your life do you enjoy? Is it financial freedom? Having loving friends or family? Do you see yourself living a better future? What is that future? Are you a living, breathing human? How do you feel on a beautiful, bright sunny day without responsibility, the sun hitting your face ever so gently, the warmth penetrating your body, lighting it up with energy? How does that make you feel? Why do you feel unloving toward yourself? Is it societal? Is it family and limiting belief systems you grew up with? Were you taught you could never be successful enough? Rich enough? Happy enough? Is it fear of failure? Money worries? Why do you feel like you're going to fail? Is it because you have in the past? Did it kill you to fail? (Obviously, it didn't.) Or did it instead lead you somewhere else? Are you really afraid of change and not failure? When have you felt like you failed before? What was the outcome of that "failure," and why did you consider it a failure? Do you STILL consider it a failure? Or did it lead you somewhere better? Do you base your successes and failures off other people's successes and failures? Are they truly yours? Can you own them? Or do you feel this way simply because it's what you were taught to believe? What is success to you? Money? (There are plenty of unhappy millionaires out there, by the way.) What does money mean to you? After all, it's only paper, but what does it signify for you? Freedom? Safety? Security? What about relationships? What is your deep-seated belief about relationships? That you're supposed to be in one? Are you feeling pressure by family and friends and feel you need to be married by a certain age? Do you believe you need to have children within a few years after that? Whose timeline is this? Is it actually yours or based on what you read about, hear about, or hear friends and family talk about? Do you tell yourself, "That's just the way it is" or "I'm just supposed to do these things" often? Do you believe those statements to be true? If yes, then by whose standards?

Do you have a headache yet? Are you sensing a pattern here? Most of the time, we live our lives through the eyes and ears of other people and not ourselves. The first step is getting back to a place where we can accept our OWN beliefs as true and OWN them.

Discover WHY you think the way you do.

"Watch what you say. You have to account for every idle word. Never say, 'I will fail; I will lose my job; I can't pay the rent.' Your subconscious cannot take a joke. It brings all these things to pass."
—Joseph Murphy

Envisioning an awesome future while still holding onto negativity will be like a sea turtle swimming through gorilla glue. You'll feel stuck. Once you learn to align your mind with your heart, you'll have an easier time; however, the issue isn't that the whole heart-mind coordination thing doesn't work. It's that most of the time when we think we're aligned, we're not. The law of attraction states that thoughts become things; however, if those thoughts are coming merely from a sense of ego and not truly your heart, this creates a disharmony between what you "think" you want and what you truly want. It's like saying you want a salad when you really want a double-bacon cheeseburger. Once you learn to dig into the deeper realms of your mind and soul, you'll be able to overcome that little voice in your head that's telling you lies.

A lot of books and movies on the law of attraction (like the *The Secret*) are great models to expand this level of thinking; however, without getting into more detail and only claiming that "thoughts become things," people either take it at face value or crank up their BS meter. The "Well, I want a million dollars, so why don't I have it yet?" type of folks come out of the woodwork. You have to dig a little deeper. Actually, you have to dig A LOT deeper. And to that man or woman who wants a million dollars: of course you want more money, but do you actually believe that you can have it? Do you feel like it's already coming into your life? Ninety-nine percent of the time, the answer is NO. Therefore, you've focused more on what you're lacking (because you're good ol' subconscious mind is playing tricks on you). Maybe you grew up in a poor to middle-class household where you were always taught that money didn't grow on trees, then went through your life as a job hopper, bouncing from place to place with the notion that in order to make money, you had to struggle like a fly on flypaper, sweat like a construction worker in 100 percent humidity, and work an eighty-hour workweek. Even then, you won't believe that you can achieve millionaire status. To you, millionaire status is strictly designated to chart-topping big-name celebrities, pro athletes with drug problems, or bigwig CEOs of pharmaceutical companies trying to steal your soul. Not you.

What is your subconscious mind telling you? Be careful … what you think you want may not be what you want at all. Are you focused on material possessions to fulfill your happiness? Do you want a million dollars because that's what everyone else in life wants? Or can you fulfill your underlying need for happiness through any other means? Wanting a million dollars could mean subconsciously that you actually want stability. Could financial stability be what you're really asking for, and is it more believable to obtain that than exactly one million bucks? Could you settle for less than a million to meet your desire? Tweak your requests based on what's going on with you subconsciously, and start there. This is just a hunch, but you might find that it's a hell of a lot easier to manifest financial stability for yourself than a million dollars. I'm not saying you can't manifest a million in your life because you absolutely can (the possibilities are infinite), but for most average folks, it's not in the cards due to limiting beliefs and what they believe they can actually achieve.

I used to tell my acupuncture patients all the time, the longer you've held on to something, usually the longer it takes to heal. That goes for your brain too. The longer your subconscious mind has been exposed and programmed to think a certain way, the longer it may take to reprogram it. It's like defragging your computer. That shit takes FOREVER, but when it's done, it's done. Clean slate. Open to new programs. If you've always thought of yourself as fat, ugly, or insecure, then you're not going to sit through a twenty-five-minute self-hypnosis session and wake up "cured." You might wake up different, but chances are, all those years of programming in your brain haven't just been erased in one shot. Life doesn't work that way, and neither does your brain.

In Dr. Joe Dispenza's book, *Breaking the Habit of Being Yourself,* he mentions that by the time we reach our mid-thirties, we basically run our brains and bodies on autopilot. This means that we've lived thirty-five years or so embedding our subconscious minds with information from our environment. We literally lose our presence and turn into zombies, although most of us never acquire the taste for human flesh (I'll stick to chicken).

Stop Rushing Through Your Life

Why do we try to rush through our lives? Where are we going? According to good ol' Albert Einstein, time is all relative depending on your placement in the Universe, gravity, speed, and a bunch of other factors. Quantum physics shows us that everything, past, present, and future, happens all at once; however, this is a hard pill to digest. It's kind of similar to the notion that we exist in 99.9 percent empty space, and everything we see, hear, or experience as solid matter is, in fact, vibrating energy. We deny it because we can't see it. We can't experience it. We don't feel the chair vibrating beneath us, we don't see our television set bopping up and down like a sixth-grade cheerleader with pom-poms, and we certainly don't observe our cluttered bedroom as "empty space," so our brains don't actually accept it. It's a big fat fairy-tale in our minds.

Energy is like an eHarmony profile. It resonates with other energy that likes the same things. We attract things into our reality that match with the vibration we're sending out. This is why for us to successfully bring our potential desires into our reality, it has to match our vibration and heartfelt desires to a T. If it doesn't, that future possibility will always exist outside the scope of reality. We won't experience it in this dimension anytime soon.

There is no rush to life. Minutes pass regardless of our perception of how fast or slow they go. The more we waste our time focusing on negative things, complaining, criticizing, and judging ourselves and others, the more we take away time we could spend actually being useful. Once we look past judgment, we truly let go and surrender to transformation. Once we learn to live out of compassion instead of anger or disgust, the greater life gets. Once we open our eyes to who we truly are and how we are connected to one another, we feel a giant weight lift off our shoulders. Suddenly, life becomes lighter, easier, smoother, and more secure. We stop experiencing fear of everyone and everything. We stop doubting ourselves. We become more stable, persevering, confident, trustful, optimistic, and ultimately fulfilled. We start taking better care of ourselves physically, emotionally, and spiritually. We find ourselves being kinder and gentler toward other human beings. And as we progress into a more compassionate, gentler state, we begin to notice that kindness and comfort comes back to us. People become nicer in our eyes, we find ourselves grateful to be experiencing life in this time and space. We focus on progressing and connecting to powers higher than ourselves while still feeling grounded. This is transformation, and while at first it can feel somewhat uncomfortable, we find ourselves in a beautiful state of being. That is transformation at its finest. And while many people may never get to experience this beautiful place and time due to their never-ending battle with themselves, you can. They may never truly awaken to life in its most genuine and vulnerable form, but you will.

We can base our lives off of money, material possessions, defining and identifying ourselves through our careers or social status, and never truly get it, this whole life and living thing. Those who do "get it" understand how other people can go through life this way, but we share and educate others just by being more compassionate, gentle, kind, and accepting of ourselves and others, living our lives from a state of gratefulness and being completely happy knowing that this is our gift to others. Some, if not many, may not see it through, but a few may, and it may change their lives in a way we may never comprehend.

So smile and say hi to someone today. Actually, make eye contact and smile at the girl pouring your morning coffee at Starbucks. Stop going through life in a fog and wake up. You have life to live. There's no need to rush through it or expect anything from anyone. Expect only greatness from yourself. Expect yourself to live with a compassion and enthusiasm for your actions. Expect the unexpected. Expect that your heart fills with joy every moment you wake up to a new day. For that is greatness. That is life. That is energy. No one can take your joy away from you. It's in your heart and always will be, even if it's deep in hiding from you right now.

The Feedback Loop of Our Minds (and How to Break Out of It)

I used to always tell myself, "Today's a new day." I'd tell myself that this was the day I was going to change, be a different person, walk a different walk, talk a different talk, and that I'd get a reflection of this in my day to prove it. I was starting anew. Brand-new and improved Jen. And then I'd find myself in a loop. It was like my body and brain were stuck on permanent autopilot. Suddenly, my world felt so small, life so insignificant. I felt trapped. There were a million different places I could travel to and a million different things I could do, yet I felt like my body wouldn't steer that way, almost like it couldn't. It felt chained, limited to only the same surroundings, the same neighborhoods, driving down the same streets, and only stopping at the same places. I was like a bad Twilight Zone episode. I had trained my mind to become so limited that

I was screaming for help inside. It had been programmed in this type of loop, and I didn't know how to break out of it. Each time I would tell myself that "Today's the day" or "I'm going to go somewhere I've never been before" or "I'm going to do something I've never done" to break free of my mind's straight jacket, I'd always revert back.

Why is it so difficult? Why are we so resistant to change in our lives? Every time we find ourselves reverting back to going off our diets, smoking that cigarette, or being too lazy to go to the gym, every time we rationalize in our heads, make excuses, go back to that relationship or that comfort food, or that job where we feel safe, we feel guilty. We feel like we've failed. We feel like there's something wrong with us. "Why do I always do this?" we ask ourselves. "I have no strength, no willpower, no perseverance, no drive, and I'll never be like 'them.' I'll always do this to myself, I'll always fail, and I'll never change."

Listen to these words. "I failed." "I'm not good enough." How many times have you told yourself these words? I bet you've probably told yourself that you "can't" more times than you've told yourself that you "can." What kind of impression do you think that has on your brain? Do you think it affects your future decisions? You betcha.

We LOVE running on autopilot mode. After all, it takes the guesswork out of being humanly responsible and gives our complex conscious minds a break. Imagine if every time you sat down and shut the door to your car, you had to retrain yourself how to drive again? It would be like driving your car for the very first time EACH AND EVERY TIME. Remember how scared you felt the first time you ever drove a car? It would be like pulling out on that busy highway for the very first time all over again. Can you imagine what it would be like if you had to feel that way every single day? Your body would be in a constant state of panic and anxiety. You'd probably want to wet your pants. So thank your brain for autopilot setting because it has its perks. Every image, sight, sound, smell, and feeling we experience from our five senses forms an imprint in our brain. And the more times we experience similar or the same things over and over again, the more that sector of our brain gets highlighted. After a while, it just becomes routine and requires no conscious thinking. We just automatically do it. So how do we change it? We reprogram it, and yes, similar to a computer.

Our Innate Fear Response

What is fear anyway? It is a state of being, an emotion that signals a red flag to our body. It tries to protect us from harm, whether that be physical or emotional. Back in the day, cavemen feared being eaten by a cave lion as they were hunting and gathering for their families. Today, we've evolved to fear more superficial things—not necessarily with putting our bodies on the line, but things like not having enough money, not getting the job we want, failing at something, fear of looking stupid, fear of being judged, and the fear of getting sick, the last one being more physical in nature. Most of us have some sort of legit excuse for our anxiety, to the point where it's one of the largest clinical-diagnosed disorders, resulting in massive amounts of medication being pumped into the world. Hundreds of years ago, something like Xanax never existed, so how did men and women who feared being eaten by a lion cope? Well, they weren't popping Xanax, that's for sure, but what they did was face their fear. They took action even though they were afraid because it was a matter of life and death. Survival. If they didn't learn to accept the fear penetrating every ounce of their being, they might not have survived. They didn't give up trying to provide for their families because the alternative was always death, either via starvation or getting eaten. I'm pretty sure most of us don't have to worry about a hyena, a wild goat, or our hamster eating us.

Instead, to us, losing money or a significant other can feel equivalent to losing a limb. It can be devastating. So we feel the fear and stay in the same routine, doing the same things we've always done, staying in the same career, dating the same types of people, and never going beyond our own limitations because, in our heads, the fear of failure is greater than risking it. We play it safe, our fears eventually subside, and nothing changes, except for the fact that the stress and anxiety from the unchanged situation keeps festering within us. We don't feel the fear anymore temporarily, but we're still in a perpetual state of stress, anxiety, and inner turmoil that will eventually seep its way outwards, maybe at an inopportune time. This can create change, yes, like being fired because we cursed out our boss, divorce because we cheated on our spouse, or even jail in extreme cases because we were so fueled up that we commit something unlawful, find a new interest in heroin, or act aggressively out of character. Some of us live in a constant state of fight-or-flight mode, which is unnatural for our bodies.

I'm not saying you're going to turn into a serial killer overnight in any sense (even serial killers have their reasons, some of which we don't understand and most likely stem from some sort of trauma or pent-up aggression). Fight-or-flight is there for protection, to help us when we're in danger, like being chased by a wild animal or a person with a knife trying to attack us, but it's a mechanism that's made for short bursts, not a constant in our lives. Once it remains constant, everything is thrown off, from our hormones to our heart rhythm to our breathing. It then can affect us physically and lead us down a path of eventual disease.

Reprogramming Yourself

Reprogramming yourself can be a pain in the ass. The subconscious mind hates change and will reject whatever you initially feed it. It acts like a big brother trying to protect you from harm and, as luck would have it, this "protection" instills fear. This is what holds us back from pursuing greatness in life. Think of the subconscious as this humongous Tupperware container including every past memory, trauma, and experience you've ever undergone; therefore, if you attempt to move out of autopilot mode, chances are you're going to experience some version of fear.

Say, for example, you've been thinking of leaving your boring old fuddy-duddy desk job to become an entrepreneur, pursuing your passion of creating an online business on nose-whistling techniques, but you're afraid you won't make enough money to pay your bills. First, ask yourself: Is this fear stemming from a belief I grew up with surrounding finances? Do I actually have only enough money in my bank account to get me into the next month? If you need to do some research as to how much money you actually have including 401(k)s and bonds and such, then do that. Many times, the reality doesn't match up to the long-held belief systems.

Next, ask yourself: What potentials are out there? Just because I want to leave my job or my relationship doesn't mean something better isn't out there waiting for me. It may take a little bit of convincing or even a little bit of time, but it also might be knocking on your door tomorrow. You really don't know. If you remain stuck and fail to see what other potentials are out there for yourself, you'll always keep repeating the same story.

Third, ask yourself: Why am I freaking out? You certainly have the power to seek out alternative positions, pursue other areas of interest, or even set up your nose-whistling technique YouTube channel well before you actually make the decision to leave your job. We have a tendency to think that we have to do things right NOW without any sort of back-up plan. We need to figure it all out TODAY because the thought crossed our mind, and if we don't have an answer this second, we beat ourselves up for it. No one says you absolutely HAVE to quit now or leave NOW (unless you really want to or feel like you really need to). Who told you it had to be instantaneous? Society? Oh, wait, maybe it's the EGO. No one is pushing you to leave anywhere. Whenever you feel rushed or pushed, it's often a projection from your own mind and not reality. The above are only a few of the many questions you should ask yourself when you recognize fear. Here are a few bonus questions you can ask:

1. *Is this fear helping or hurting me?*
2. *What is the worst thing that can happen?*
3. *What is the best thing that can happen?*

Once you've recognized what you ACTUALLY feel, think, and act toward your situation, it's time to implement new data into the computer. Ask yourself: "What would I rather feel? What would I rather think? How would I rather behave?" Once you've identified a new feeling, thought, and behavior, then you can start implementing these into your subconscious mind. Basically, there are two ways to do it: aggressively or passively. Aggressively is to fight the fear head on, and passively is through slower techniques like guided meditation, visualization techniques, or hypnosis, among others. Both ways will work, but the first step is to become aware of what you're actually fearing. You have to peel the layers of the onion before you can start shifting yourself.

What is something you can do today that breaks the fear cycle in your life? There is no shame in asking for help, ever. Maybe for you, it's meditation or self-hypnosis. These are all ways to start breaking out of fear patterns that have been holding you back. If talking about it doesn't relieve some of your fears, next is resorting to more uncomfortable measures, such as fearing something and doing it anyway. Actually, this is the number one way to conquer a fear: face it head-on. Action is energy in motion, so if you're holding onto repressed emotions, moving toward it rather than away from it is the fastest track to overcoming it. It might take every ounce of your will to do so, but it can be a game changer afterward. Often, this is one of the most difficult actions to take, but if you can take a deep breath, suck it up, and remind yourself you're not going to lose your life over it (unless you've decided to try jumping across mountains freestyle, which I wouldn't necessarily recommend), you'll be okay. In fact, you'll be more than okay after it's over and done with.

Fear of Change Is Inside Us All

Sometimes, when we start seeing sudden changes in our life, fear kicks into high gear. We start doubting ourselves. We question things and whether or not we actually possess the ability to succeed. We begin wondering if we even want what we want anymore. We say to ourselves, "This is what I wanted, and now that I'm starting to see things happening around me, I'm not so sure." We completely freak out when things start shifting. Why? Well, take comfort in knowing that you are 100 percent normal. If you didn't experience any amount of doubt, then I might assume you're straight from George Jetson's living room. Fear is normal. It's normal to feel it when we're out of our element. We fear the unknown. We fear the future. We fear failing. Name one person who hasn't experienced fear before? The key is to recognize fear for what it is—an emotion. The real question is: What will you do with fear? Will you let it overpower and overwhelm you? Will you let it sink its grimy teeth in you and cause those little negative monsters of your ego to keep hashing over things that haven't happened or may not ever happen?

We fear failure because we're taught to fear failure. As kids, we're taught that getting a bad report card, missing a layup in basketball, or making only minimum wage in a job isn't good enough. We're taught to live in fear by the media. We're too fat, we're not pretty enough, strong enough, smart enough, or healthy enough to survive. Therefore, we need this diet, fitness program, movie series, product, or drug to feel better. We need new makeup or wrinkle-smoothing skin cream, we won't have enough money for retirement or to buy a new car, the government is out to get us, companies are out to screw us, natural disasters are becoming worse by the minute, everyone is selfish and corrupt, rapists, murderers, drug dealers, and gunslingin' rednecks are all out running loose, so you better not go to the movies for fear of getting shot, abused, injected with poison, or find yourself in an earthquake. Whew … did I miss anything?

The media almost never focuses on anything positive (as you're probably already aware), with the exception of a few fluffy stories here and there for puffery. But honestly, who wants to read and hear about the man who helped me carry my groceries to my car and helped me unload a forty-eight-pack of Costco bottled water into my trunk? Lame-o is the name-o. Sincerity just doesn't sell these days. Sex and violence, on the other hand, that does.

It's not that everything is spoiled meat. Honestly, I think society as a whole, and human beings as a species, are shifting and waking up. People are getting tired of the negativity and trying to focus on more positive things. Why? It's because people are finally realizing that positivity is like a dose of sunshine on a warm summer day. It just feels better. It's like a Deepak Chopra book tattooed onto our brain. It's like a kid with a McDonald's Happy Meal. It's a relief to have positive vibes floating around like a bunch of jumbo-sized fluffy cotton balls.

It gives me a flashback to the time I was sitting at the Barnes & Noble café (where I used to do most of my writing), and the young man working behind the counter was obviously having a rough day. I could see he was flustered and anxious, and I must have heard him apologize at least once or twice to every single customer after me. For the short time I was there, he managed to spill someone's change all over the counter and floor, knocked scalding hot coffee all over this woman's shirt (lawsuit much?), pronounced everyone's name ridiculously wrong (including mine … because "Jen" is so often mispronounced), had difficulty scanning a multitude of items, messed up someone's cupcake order, pissed off a young kid who only had a half-hour lunch break and had been waiting for three quarters of that time for a muffin and coffee, and went in the back to ask his manager for advice at least ten times. I had only been there twenty minutes, and he had managed to do how many things wrong? I felt bad, actually. If he had stopped, taken a breath for even two minutes, I imagine his whole afternoon might have changed. However, he chose to live off of fumes in his head, in a constant state of fight-or-flight that was lingering still from that initial anxious encounter. He had focused on everything he had done wrong, and the law of attraction responded appropriately.

It's like one of those days where you wake up, your coffee isn't hot enough (I know, real-world problems right there), and you DECIDE that the rest of your day is going to be that way. You get out of bed, stub your toe on the dresser, then sulk all the way to the kitchen. You then proceed to burn your toast, drop a glob of peanut butter on your blouse, break your shoelace AND the zipper on your pants (thus sobbing over how much peanut butter you ate), then you rush off to your car, dropping your keys in the very same puddle you just stepped in. Driving on your way to work, you happen to get every single red light, thus arriving late to the office. This leads you to miss your mandatory morning staff meeting, whereby you get scolded by your boss, develop a stomach ache from your curry chicken lunch, get stuck with extra work because your client emails you at 4:55 p.m. to fix an error you made previously on a document, then you unfortunately get in a fender bender on your way home because you weren't paying attention. You end up stopping at Mickey D's for a cheeseburger because you're STARVING and end up eating a squished, tasteless stale burger in which they forgot to add the cheese. You proceed to pull into your driveway, get out of your car (noticing the newly dented bumper), and arrive inside your house welcomed by a pool of your dog's stinky diarrhea all over your clean floors. Oh yeah, did I mention you accidentally stepped in it on your way in? Yeah, that type of day.

If you subconsciously think it's going to be a hell of a day, then you better believe it'll be a hell of a day. If you're constantly afraid of failing, then failing is what you'll experience the more you focus on it.

Some ways around this (and there are ways around this):

1. **Focus on what was good about your day.**
    What were your strengths today? How was your general mood? Were your words positive and uplifting, or did you spend a majority of your day apologizing to others for things you think you failed at? Focus on the little wins instead of the big losses. Your reality is a reflection of your attention, so start finding the advantages in everyday things.

2. **Embrace the fear. Then let it go.**
    We all experience fear, but the minute you dwell on it is the minute it balloons out of proportion to reality. Attaching to fear is dwelling. Observe the fear, say hello to it, give it a hug, then let that shit go. It's okay to embrace it. In fact, you should, but there's a huge difference between embracing it and suffocating it, between observing and dwelling. Fear is not the enemy. Your reaction to fear is the enemy.

3. **Even if you've had a really bad day, it doesn't mean you'll have a bad night.**
    We control our thought energy. Our thought energy controls our reality. Essentially, we attract what

we're mostly thinking about. So instead of always throwing up your hands in a dramatic fashion and screaming to yourself, *"AHH THIS DAY IS HELL! I GIVE UP!"* you think instead, *"Okay, now's my golden opportunity to turn this sad little puppy around and have a fan-fucking-tabulous night. Let's go!"* you invite in a better time.

Fear Often Hides in the Not-So-Obvious Places

The cause of our fears is usually a combination of what we're taught growing up by parents, peers, other dominant adult figures, and society. In some cases, we're not even aware of what we're fearing. We're bombarded with television commercials, movies, books, social media, and advertising (often all are one and the same). Our subconscious minds pick up on this information and we begin holding onto certain fears like a newborn clinging to its mother's nipple.

How do we break the mold of fear-based actions? For starters, **pay attention.** Pay attention to what you see and hear on television, in commercials, what you read in magazines, and what advertising is trying to sell you. AWARENESS IS KEY. Most television commercials and magazine ads are not out for your highest good but for the single purpose of making you feel like crap. They make you feel like you have some sort of problem that needs to be fixed, and the only way to fix it is by buying a certain product or service. They want you scared. So become aware of the news outlets you're watching, how often you're watching them, and what the underlying meaning is. You'll notice (if you haven't already) that a good percentage of the stories or ads are almost always fear based. Here's a news flash. **The world really is not quite as bad as it's portrayed on television.** There are plenty of loving, empowering, amazing people out there whom you can and should trust. You don't need to walk around feeling that you have to carry an assault rifle on you at all times. That is fear. If you're constantly watching war movies, horror movies, and THE NEWS for five hours a day, followed by your nighttime crime dramas, all while scrolling on social media, reading a magazine, AND yesterday's newspaper, then you are not only great at multitasking, but you're also injecting your subconscious brain with fear-based information and entertainment.

So how much is too much? Where is the cut off between staying informed and overloading your brain to the point where fear overwhelms you? Take a look at the way you think. How do you feel every morning when you wake up? How do you feel as you're interacting with people throughout the day? Where are you spending your time other than work (if you work)? Are you spending three-plus hours watching television, plus two hours on your phone, mindlessly scrolling through angry political posts? How are you bettering yourself as a person? *Are* you bettering yourself as a person?

Let me clarify. These aren't question to intimidate you or make you feel bad about yourself. These are questions to get to know what you're feeling and where you're actually spending a majority of your time. What are you doing RIGHT NOW that is making you a better human being? Well, umm, yes, you're reading this book, but I mean in a general sense. How are you living your current reality that is improving you as a person? Benefitting YOU. Not someone else, but YOU. If your answer is vague or if your answer is "Jen … I'm scrolling through my Facebook newsfeed every day while sitting in front of the boob tube eating my Pringles potato chips," then how is this making you a better person? Not that there's anything wrong with this scenario AT ALL. (One of my favorite things to do some nights is to pour myself a Jen-sized glass of wine and sit my ass in front of the TV, but I also make sure I balance it with bettering myself by meditating, exercising, eating healthier food, and limiting my screen time.) BUT, is this your go-to activity for the day? Are you coming home from work exhausted and want to do nothing more with your life than plop on the couch? If you're okay with this, then that's perfectly cool, but if there's always been something in the back of your mind urging you to live with more purpose, then it's important that you tap into and listen to that urge. If you didn't have an urge, you wouldn't be inclined to buy self-help books. If every square inch of you were 100 percent whole and complete, you wouldn't be reading this right now. See what I mean? There's comfort and then there's settling for less.

Start your day with something positive

The fact of the matter is, we're addicted to our devices. It's difficult not to check our phones as soon as we wake up, check our email at breakfast, or scroll through our newsfeeds while drinking our morning cup of coffee. We're bombarded twenty-four seven by technology, so why not start the day without it? Getting up first thing in the morning and automatically turning on your phone and checking your email or social media is setting yourself up for anxious thoughts. You're bound to see something you don't like, and on a subconscious level, you start inviting in negative emotions. You invite anxiety into your day before it's even necessary.

To be honest, I used to buy the newspaper almost every day, but most mornings I'd find myself reading the comics section instead of the actual news (it's my primary reason for buying newspapers now). The way I see it, I'd like to start my day off with some Dagwood and Ziggy over who was found guilty of rape, murder, and the obituaries, but that's just me. Beginning your day with something positive not only feels better, but it has a tendency to extend into the rest of your day. They say that breakfast is the most important meal of the day, or at least they used to (before intermittent fasting became cool). Well, your morning routine is the most important time of the day, in my opinion. There's something about the morning … cool, crisp air, wet dew on the grass, vivid colors, the calm before the storm of traffic and sirens, and it's also the perfect time to infuse your brain with positivity that will carry over into the rest of your day.

Taking a Break

Sometimes breaks are crucial. For example, taking a break from writing once in a while certainly doesn't mean that I don't like writing anymore; it just means that I need a small breather. A chance to recharge or mix things up is never a bad thing. In fact, it's good for the soul, and it's certainly good for the brain. Over time, we create new patterns in our brain based on our experiences. Think of your daily routine. You wake up, you use the bathroom, most likely, you drink your coffee, maybe you exercise, you eat the same old boring oatmeal topped with the same tablespoon and a half of raw walnuts with eight ounces of almond milk, topped with exactly three dashes of cinnamon and one dash of nutmeg. Then maybe you brush your teeth, you get dressed, you meditate or check your emails, you get in your car, then you drive to work, where you do the same job you did yesterday, you eat the same boring salad with chicken for lunch, you drink the same type of tea in the afternoon, you have the same conversations with the same people, you drive home from work, you take the dog out (if you have one), you make dinner for yourself or your family, you unwind for a bit and watch television or read a good book, then you go to bed only to wake up seven or eight hours later to do the same exact thing all over again. If this doesn't sound so bad, it doesn't have to be. A lot of people are very comfortable in their routine, BUT what makes it uncomfortable for some are the ones who want more.

When you go against the grain and start adding new things into your routine (say you decide to eat steak for breakfast and go outdoors for a walk instead of the treadmill in your basement, or maybe you decide to take a personal day from work and go to a museum instead), this begins a rewiring of your brain. Now you start creating new experiences, circuits, and new neural pathways. It's like inputting new data into a computer instead of working with outdated software. It's only when you repeatedly do different things, meet new people, visit new locations, and learn new things over time that you create, essentially, a new you.

Sounds easy, right? Well, in theory it is. The issue, however, is that our brain also releases chemicals based on how we feel, so when we suddenly try to change the atmosphere, the body always wants to revert back to what it knows and considers safe. This is why negative people or those who have suffered a lot of trauma in their lives may find it difficult to put on an external happy face for long periods of time. It's the same as training a muscle. The more you train your bicep, the stronger it gets with time; however, if you only trained your bicep once or twice, then gave up entirely, what would happen? Your bicep would weaken and shrink back to its original size. If you want to lose fifty pounds, you can't just diet for one day. You need to remain on a consistent regimented exercise and nutrition schedule for an extended period of time. And even after you've lost the weight, you have to remain in some sort of continual program and nutrition lifestyle to sustain the healthy weight loss. However, it's much easier to sustain the weight loss than to initially lose the weight because we've already begun the process of changing the brain patterning. It's like meditation. It always seems more difficult to find the patience to meditate for ten minutes the first time you do it, but over time, it becomes a habit and just another part of your daily routine.

Success is Not Monetary

My family has always had this grand vision of me working for a pharmaceutical company or at a hospital where I could get a well-paying full-time gig with benefits. This was a "real job" by my father's standards. I think he's always thought that this would solve all of my problems, and I could qualify as successful as some of my cousins who work nine-to-five jobs with health benefits and 401(k). I've done the gig, I know what it's like, and sure it would be easier to fall into that sort of thing, but would I be happier just because of the financial stability? Not necessarily.

Why live life feeling miserable or unhappy? I've always thought this way. We spend a majority of our days working for money to get where exactly? So many people in this world work to make a decent living, pay their bills, put away money for retirement, but spend the majority of their time miserable.

They never enjoy the fruits of their labor. They hate their jobs. They do the same things day after day. They don't live with purpose. They are asleep at the wheel of their own lives and don't even realize it. I don't believe we should just keep going and repeating the same patterns of trying to make ends meet day after day and never get to enjoy 75 to 100 percent of our lives. Is there a point to that? We might as well love what we do 75 to 100 percent of the time. Otherwise, we go against our true nature—following our heart, living in alignment, embracing life, and all that jazz. We are NOT our jobs, and we are NOT our status. Sure, money is awesome and I suppose I could just get a "job" at a pharmaceutical company or hospital or something (maybe) and try to be happy about it, but how far would that happiness take me if it wasn't truly aligned with my real purpose here on earth or not in line with what I actually wanted to do in life? I could tell myself that I'm happy because I make enough money, have a solid 401(k) plan, full benefits and all the perks, but then what? What happens when that elation wears down? What comes after me being able to afford more and more stuff? What would I be left with? Perhaps an unfulfilling life is what I'm thinking. This isn't the land of make-believe either. This is how a lot of people live. They become stuck in this loop of status, money, ego, and frustration. Once they're in, it's difficult to get out because they've entered the comfort zone. It's almost like the Twilight Zone, but much worse. In it, they lose a sense of purpose and true self.

The ego is responsible for a lot of not-so-great things in life. Maybe you want to live your life thinking that money is the only answer to all your problems, and that's totally fine. Have at it. You might not be reading this book if you actually thought that, though. I'm just sayin'. Not to be morbid, but do me a favor and think of a time when someone close to you is dying or dies. Is the first thought that comes to mind, "OMG! Funeral expenses!" or is it a more heart-felt emotion like sadness or love? If it's the first answer, then I'd assume that this person was not truly close to you because if it were your mother or your sister or something, you might do the freak-out about the money AFTER your initial reaction, which implies that the money is NOT the most important thing in your life.

We all have a drive in us. We just need to discover it instead of letting others dictate our true life path.

We Can Learn A lot from Guinea Pigs (Running Away from Our Problems)

Sometimes I look at my guinea pigs, Albert and Wolfgang, and I wonder what goes through their tiny little brains. Guinea pigs are anxious rodents by nature. Poor things—their only defensive mechanism is running away because they think everyone and everything is a predator (including my hand). Yet they are such loveable creatures. We could say the same for people. We can be so loveable yet so annoyingly fearful. And I'm talking about everything. While we tend to prey on each other, we have the same basic instinct to run away once fear kicks in. Once we realize we might fail at something, we book it. We distract ourselves with cute little guinea pig and cat videos on YouTube (which is perfectly acceptable, by the way), we avoid situations that might hurt us, we resort to substances or comfort foods to alter our minds and feed our woes. We do it all because it's ingrained in every one of us, some more than others.

So what happens when we try breaking this habit/streak for ourselves? Our bodies and our minds want to resort back to the only thing we know: the big squishy couch of our comfort zone.

All my life, I've been great at avoiding. I've avoided people and uncomfortable situations and circumstances out of pure fear. I have a fear of failure, responsibility, and a fear of opening myself up to others. Avoiding people and situations is a way for me to take my control back. Taking the easy road, I guess you could say. I'm the chicken in that fourth-grade drug Public Service Announcement that's too scared to puff on a cigarette, except I'm scared to death of failing at life. We all are, to a certain degree. The truth of the matter is that avoidance gets us nowhere fast in life. It might temporarily distract us or make things easier, but it always ends up backfiring because we can only avoid for so long. We may even end up worse off than if we confronted our fears right in the face. We're scared. We feel like it's easier not to deal with something that makes us uncomfortable. However, our comfort zone can become our safety net for so long before we need to do something to move past it.

Excuses

I used to keep a diary. Looking back at one of the entries I wrote years ago, I came to one conclusion: I used to make a lot of excuses. I had written about how tired I felt because I played an ice hockey game the night before; I had gone to bed too late because my team and I all went out to a bar for dinner afterwards, and I didn't feel like writing that particular day because I was having a "low vibe" day because I didn't get to bed until almost midnight the night before. I was snacking because I was tired, then it had an effect on my blood sugar, which made me tired and cranky.

Did I really need to re-emphasize and write down how tired I was? Then I went to bed irritated because I had been tired of feeling tired because I snacked and went to bed late the night before, which I knew would make me tired? Are you catching my drift here? I was getting a headache just reading it. My brain had literally rationalized every single reason for me NOT to have energy. And by writing it down, I had definitely sealed the deal. Okay, I was tired, but I had to go on and on and on.

This is what the brain does. If we feel bad for not doing something or slack off in some way, we'll find excuses to get us out of the thing we don't want to do but think we should be doing. It makes us feel better if we rationalize it. It makes it more acceptable for us to be lazy. As long as we've found the excuse, we're good to not do that thing we don't want to do. The human brain is funny that way. Humans are funny that way. We'll always find every excuse in the book to validate how crappy we feel. We feel the need to yell it from the rooftops, proclaiming it to the world (or in a notebook, in my case). That makes it okay. Yet how many times do we proclaim how ridiculously happy we are? Like, never. Okay, maybe sometimes we do, but by nature we want attention. Babies cry when they're hungry or something is bothering them. They laugh when they're happy. The only difference between babies and adults is spoken word. (And maybe the physical height differences.) What we speak about, we bring about. Whenever we put our thoughts to paper or spoken word, we give that thought more power. USE YOUR WORDS WISELY. Think before you speak. Words can be used for good or they can be used for evil. If you're constantly putting yourself down, putting down others, saying how corrupt the world is, how greedy people are, etc., then congratulations. You just made this your reality.

STEP #4

Recognize that you have the power to choose your reality.

"You experience the world not as it is, but as you are."
—Frederick Dodson

Believe it or not, you always have choice. Just like you have a choice of which pair of pants you put on each morning, you always have a choice in your actions. Sometimes we think we don't have a choice; this is where limiting beliefs come in. We say that we're stuck in a job, a relationship, a family situation, or a financial situation, but the truth is, we're never actually stuck. We tell ourselves we're stuck because we don't see any way out. There's ALWAYS a way out. Of course, the way out may not be an easy one. Take, for example, a wife who feels enslaved by her abusive husband. She feels like if she were to escape, she risks losing her life or those of her children. This is an extreme example of feeling like there's no way out; however, the fact that we cannot predict the future means that she can't predict exactly how things will pan out. Yes, she may be risking her own life by escaping, but at the same time, she is risking her own life by staying with an abusive husband. Her limiting beliefs have created a story in her mind that the only way she'll ever escape is through death. This just isn't the case, as there are many women who have managed to escape these types of situations in their lives. Was it easy? Definitely not. Was it scary? Absolutely. Did they lose their life or run into a brick wall? No, because they came to realize that they aren't the only ones going through this and there are people in the world who are waiting to help them break free. They first need to break free of their own mind and believe it's possible to actually make it possible.

Thoughts Create Reality: Desire (Wishing and Wanting) vs. Intention (Doing and Being)

We desire a lot of things in life, mostly because other people have them. The reason we want a nice BMW, a big house, more money, and more stuff in general is because other people have them. Status + Ego = showing off. We think BMW = money = success, and old 1978 station wagon = shit mobile. We compare ourselves constantly without even realizing it. Look how much social media platforms like Facebook and Instagram have taken off. It's because we can show off what we have and what we've done, often on a subconscious level to make other people jealous. Of course, I'm lumping everyone into one big pile of superficiality. Not everyone goes on social media to show off. And not everyone is focused purely on status, money, and "stuff," but take a look at how many people are. As humans, it makes us feel good to show off a little, to get sympathy when we feel like we need it, play the victim when we want the attention, to make money off other people's flaws or faults (I'll blame advertising media on this one), and make ourselves look good. Let me ask you: Are you in this lump sum, or do you have more to offer the world?

I've always had hope for myself. I've always wanted to do great things, and deep down, I knew I would do great things with my life. I wanted to be an author, an expert in my field, changing and inspiring lives. I always told myself that if I could just get past my laziness streak I had going, I would do all those things. I knew I could be inspired if the mood struck, but I wanted it to be all the time. I also realized that I didn't really like being alone at night. I know—different topic, but legit. Part of it made me feel afraid or left out.

I have fears. I have self-esteem issues like the rest of them. I care too much what others think. Once I stop caring completely, I'll be free. This is what I told myself for years. Once I'm not afraid of failure anymore and instead thrive in uneasy situations, I 'll be freakin' unstoppable. Once I get out of my own head and actually do something constructive, I will own success. These were all things I told myself every single day. These were also excuses that kept me in my comfort zone. As long as I put my goals ahead of me in the future, I'd be safe from harm. As long as things would be okay "one day," I wouldn't have to try so hard. As long as I kept these in the back of my mind, I wouldn't have to take action. They were, after all, for another day. These were the same things that kept me stuck, however.

I always loved reading books on the same topics all the time. I secretly always wanted to be the one who wrote one of the books I read. I'd rather read than write because writing requires more effort. That was my excuse for not going ahead and becoming an author for a long time.

Many people live in the reality where the world is going to hell, a reality where we'll never have enough money because rich people are greedy and evil, a reality where we'll never own a Mercedes or Ferrari or go to fancy-schmancy restaurants because it costs too much, and we don't fit in with those greedy bastards; we'll never live in a huge house with four garages, or become famous for our creativity; we'll always live in a state of lack; we'll come home from our mediocre job that pays the bills, turn on the news, and plant ourselves in front of the television for hours, complaining of the latest political blunder, the latest storm a-brewin', all while eating our Yodels and complaining that we'll never be able to lose weight. Basically, we live a reality of feeling stuck. My friend, you are not stuck.

Persistence and Patience

We love flip-flopping. And I don't mean walking in flimsy three-dollar sandals at the beach. We love pursuing our dreams until we become impatient. Then we give up. We start looking at the clock and saying to ourselves, "Well, where is it, Universe? I asked, and I'm still waiting." We literally spend years of our lives waiting ... waiting for something better to come along, waiting to be discovered, waiting to be acknowledged and accepted, and waiting for happiness to fall on our laps. The truth is, if you spend your time waiting for something better, you might spend your entire life just ... waiting. Waiting = that thing is in the future and not in your life right now. Therefore, the Universe grants your wish.

We think that now isn't the right time to pursue our dreams. We tell ourselves that once things settle down or once we have our financials in order, then maybe we'll pursue our dreams. We say, "Maybe someone will come along to sweep me off my feet," or "I'll start this writing project once my house is clean," and we never actually take action. We procrastinate like an eighth grader studying for final exams.

I have news: there will never be a good time to pursue your dreams. There will always be some sort of excuse you can come up with for not getting started. There really is no such thing as the perfect time, which is why getting started now is crucial. Taking that first step is probably the most difficult one, but over time, it builds momentum and gets easier. If you spend your life waiting on an opportunity to fall onto your lap or waiting for a perfect time, your dream will remain only a dream. Small daily actions have a compound effect over time. Why? Because taking an action every single day moves you one step closer to your ideal life. Not taking action leaves you at a standstill.

Give Your Dreams a Fighting Chance

The key is to fall in love with the journey instead of letting it frustrate you. Allow yourself to celebrate the lessons along the way. Allow yourself to embrace the ebbs and flows of your life, for this is what makes you human, beautifully complex by design. Your dreams will come to fruition if you put your intention and action into it, but the moment you doubt yourself is the moment you create resistance. Again, this has to do with that annoying self-gratification thing we learned throughout our life.

Read the Right Books Instead of Being a Social Media Zombie

Fill your brain with knowledge. Self-help can actually become a detriment to your potential because if you don't utilize the techniques laid out in one book before you're already on to the next one, you may be addicted. You like the temporary high an inspiring book gives you, but if you're not applying the principles, not much will change. So if you're going to read books, make sure you either use the techniques laid out in them, read books on other subjects (maybe learn something new), or write your own damn book.

Social media isn't all evil, but it definitely has the potential to make you impatient and anxious. Scrolling on Instagram or Facebook at night and watching people fight with online trolls, while it can be fun from time to time, is also a waste of your time. Particularly before bed, you want to fuel your brain with positive things, not some political drama online. Never go to bed angry. Never. Read a few pages of a book after you wake up and before you go to sleep. The secret is to keep reminding yourself of good habits, so make sure what you read is beneficial. *The Bloody Bible Camp Massacre* may not be the best choice before bed. Reading books on personal development, law of attraction, positive thinking, subconscious programming, quantum physics, and reality creation have not only helped me maintain a positive mindset, but they have expanded my thinking. I found that doing this makes you more conscious, and you're suddenly more aware when you have a negative thought. Instead of just letting it creep up on you automatically, taking you on the merry-go-round of despair, insecurity, and depression, suddenly you feel like you have a choice. Sure, you can hop on that slippery slope, but one time, you may choose not to. Eventually, one time turns into two times into three times into forty-five, and so on. The more aware you are of your thinking, the more ability you have to choose new thoughts.

Surround Yourself with Happy, Peppy People

Through meet-up groups, attending seminars of motivational speakers or your favorite authors, or starting your own friend's circle or online support group, you can meet some pretty amazing folks. Believe me, it may not seem like it, but I guarantee there are a lot of freaking happy people out there. Even if the news says there aren't. For example, I have a friend, Amanda, whom I've known since kindergarten. I consider her a "fire starter" friend because she's the type of person to always ignite a fire under my ass and never fails to inspire me to take action or pursue my dreams. So surround yourself with more Amandas or people who fit the description. After all, you are the summary of the five people you hang out with the most. I don't even see her that often, but every once in a while, it's like I get a little "tune up" of motivation.

Write It Out

Write out those negative thoughts as they are happening. You might become really surprised how silly some of them seem. For example, I remember looking back through old journal entries to days when I was feeling extremely low (maybe some from hormones, not really sure), and I had to laugh at how utterly depressing I sounded in some of them. If I only had a big bowl of buttery popcorn and cheese doodles for the pity party I threw for myself, it would've been a win-win.

My point is that writing it all down brings some perspective and light to a situation. In retrospect, you'll often notice how your life "completely sucks" or how "worthless" you are one day, then the next you realize, "Hmm ... okay, maybe I don't actually want to ship myself off to another planet because I love my kitty cat Jezebel and my aloe plant waaay too much."

"But Jen," you ask, "how do I know if I've changed my subconscious belief patterns?" Well, for starters, you'll just feel a little better, a little more grounded, a little more optimistic, and a little more compassionate toward others and yourself.

You may even start enjoying your life and the present moment a little more. You might even smile at people more often. You'll know when you want to move on to greener pastures. There's really no rule book or time frame laid out to move to the next step.

Focus on the Feeling, Then Let That Shit Go

I am guilty. *Raises hand.* I've read every law of attraction book on the market, listened to TONS of meditations and self-hypnosis recordings. I even held every manifestation crystal, lathered myself in Abundance essential oils, wrote out hundreds of lame-sounding affirmations, and stuff still wasn't showing up. Why? I was literally trying too hard. I wasn't allowing. I wasn't letting shit go. I wasn't trusting the Universe's great skills. And I surely wasn't helping myself by becoming frustrated because of it. So what did I do differently? First of all, I stopped checking my emails on my phone so damn much. I went to the park to watch the ducks instead. I stopped spending half my day wondering whether today would be the day for a new opportunity to show itself. I stopped waiting on other people. Instead, I started focusing on the happy little trees in my life … the true joys. I'd ask myself: "What can I do today that makes me happy?" No, I didn't give up on my dreams. I still kept the routine of daily meditation, visualizing my dream life, and I took some sort of action every single day. I kept these habits as simple and easy as brushing my teeth and then I let it all go. I stopped obsessing and placing excess importance on my dreams. THAT was the difference that changed my life.

TRUST THE PROCESS. Everyone who is more successful than us *always* tells us to "trust the process, trust the process," TRUST. THE. PROCESS. But can we actually 100 percent trust the process? After all, we're putting the work in, so why isn't anything happening? The truth is, things ARE happening. You either don't see them yet, or things are happening but not as you anticipated. Why? Take a look again. If you're focusing so much on what's NOT happening and why it's NOT happening, you are once again focused from the "I'm lacking" point of view. It's that simple ... yet it's complex. Give up trying so hard. Yes, I give you permission. You need to give yourself permission, though; that's the key. Seriously, go take a walk, go for a drive, and tune yourself out for a while. Sometimes we try so hard to make something happen that we're trying to force-feed the Universe. The Universe just doesn't respond to force. In fact, it doesn't like it and will often give you the opposite. The Universe responds to an intention backed by an emotion, so if you're always whining in your head about the things that haven't come into fruition in your life, always complaining that things will never change for you no matter how many affirmations you write down or listen to, what you're projecting is frustration, disappointment, and negativity. Guess what these emotions attract? More of the same ... more disappointment, more frustration, and more negativity. Instead, you have to come from that place in your heart, a place of gratitude, a place of true knowing and belief that you already have what it is that you desire. You can live presently and still believe you have abundance. You can live presently and still become excited that new opportunities are on their way or already knocking at your door. You can live presently as a healthy, sexy, amazing individual.

Sometimes it's also a matter of tweaking your intention. Give the Universe some leeway as opposed to limiting yourself or becoming too much of a dictator (e.g., "Dear Universe.

I want my boss, Pablo, to give me a forty-thousand-dollar raise within the next week; otherwise, I disown you. Love, Jen"). Perhaps your boss Pablo will provide you with a raise eventually, but you need to believe it in order to see it. Perhaps you believe that Pablo will provide a raise, but maybe not forty thousand dollars and not in the same week. Focus on feeling abundant first instead of the number amount. Abundance can come in any form, not just forty thousand dollars, and not just from your job. By being too directive, you actually limit yourself in terms of bringing things into your reality. If you narrow down your intention so much, the window of opportunity is that much smaller. It's okay to be specific, but not to the point where it's the ONLY way you see things happening.

You need to work the law of attraction in stages. See, a lot of us THINK we want something, but in truth, it's not actually what we want. It's what other people want. It's what society wants for us. For the longest time I'd meditate daily, trying to manifest what I thought was the job of my dreams (I was specific about locations, hours, days of the week, pay, etc.), and while this might have worked for someone else, why didn't it work for me? Because subconsciously it's not what I truly wanted for myself. It's what I THOUGHT I wanted, but delving deeper, I uncovered that I wanted the job because I felt financially insecure. I wanted more money not because I felt like I truly needed it, but because it was my limiting belief system ingrained since birth. My mentality was that "money solves all problems," and "you aren't successful unless you make a lot of money." I'd hear my father's voice in my head.

You'll always have people, family, friends, etc. who will find fault in your choices. Often times this stems from our own lack of self-esteem, but once you figure out those underlying subconscious beliefs, you owe it to yourself to overcome them. How do you overcome them? Quite frankly, you don't even try. You don't react. You don't fight with them. Essentially, you do your own thing.

Always Wishing for the Past or the Future

By nature, we're wishful thinkers. When we're kids, we wish we were adults. When we're adults, we wish we were kids again. As a kid, we wanted to be like the grownups and be able to go to bed and eat ice cream whenever we wanted, and maybe even drink that red stuff or yellow stuff (that slightly resembled urine) that all the adults seemed to love, sometimes in super fancy glasses or frosty thick glass mugs they clunked together. And then we become adults, and suddenly it doesn't feel as freeing anymore. We wish we could limit our dessert intake, drink less wine, go to bed earlier, and have less responsibility. We wish someone would take care of us again. We wish we could play again and find the fun in the little things like Matchbox cars, Lincoln Logs, or board games like Candyland. Yet maybe we'd still find fun in those things, but we don't allow ourselves to experience them again. I don't have kids, but I'm certain there are a lot of parents out there who would rather stay home with their kids making fake siren engine noises and pushing along a pink plastic Barbie BMW rather than go to work. Unfortunately, adult toys just get more and more expensive … flat-screen TVs, cars, iPhones, and a bunch of other gadgets we don't really need for survival. Suddenly, our fun revolves around waiting around for the weekend to binge-watch old episodes of Dawson's Creek on the couch.

It's easy to dismiss our creativity, our oomph for life, and why is that? It's because we plug ourselves into this narrow little socket where the connection is so weak that the light shows up dim. It flickers from time to time (we all have these moments of truth where we feel alive). The question I want to ask you is, do you feel ALIVE?

Sure, you're breathing, you can see stuff, you can walk, you can talk, and you can even roll your tongue into a little hot dog shape. But do you feel *alive* alive? How many times per day do you feel sensation in your body? How many times are you really living in the present moment? What is presence, really? How many moments of the day are you thinking of nothing but these words without your brain making some sort of connection to something you said or did in the past or something you should, could, or will do, say, think, feel, or hear? Can you honestly say that RIGHT now your brain isn't thinking about anything else in connection to these words?

See, we think we're living in the present even when we're not. We think we're not thinking about other stuff when, in fact, we are. This is why something like meditation is called a practice because it's difficult to undo twenty, thirty, forty, or fifty years of thinking way too damn much.

STEP #5

Make the conscious choice to align with your Ideal Reality.

*"Any given moment contains unlimited futures
that can become real.
The reality that occurs is the one you
pay attention to."*
—Penney Peirce

If I told you that you already had the life of your dreams, would you believe me? Chances are, you wouldn't. What I want to tell you is this: what you desire for your life already exists. That version of you living the high life? It already exists. That 2.0 version of you living in a mansion or having the job or relationship of your dreams? It's already there. The issue? You can't see it. Quite simple, you aren't in vibrational alignment with it yet. All that is, was, or ever will be exists in something called a "quantum field." This is almost like a matrix (if you've seen the movie) where all possibilities exist. You can tap into one of these possibilities at any time, but you have to be in complete alignment with it first. It's like you're tuned to 101.5 FM, and your dream life is tuned to 93.3 FM. You have to keep tweaking the radio station to get it right, meaning you have to tune your own body's frequency to 93.3 FM in order to bring it into your physical reality.

Raising Your Vibration to What You Want

Since we've already discussed what energy is and how we vibrate as human beings, let's talk about specific ways to raise your vibration to get you into alignment with what you want in your life. As human beings, we actually have a very high natural frequency. The key, however, is to maintain it. We find ourselves dipping into the pool of negativity more often than we'd like, exposing ourselves to the people, places, and things that keep us in a low state. This is often why we don't see what we want because we're too low on the vibrational scale. We often wade in emotions like fear, anger, or guilt, preventing us from tuning to our favorite radio station (in this case, 93.3 FM) where our dream life actually exists. It's through these physical, environmental, or emotional influences that we feel disconnected from our true high state. On the contrary, there's hope! There are a number of ways to remain in a higher state, some of which I've listed below:

1. **Limit your exposure to energy vampires and other negative influences in your life.** You've all witnessed an energy vampire at one time or another in your life, I'm sure. These are people who literally suck the life out of your energy while hanging out with them. They could be family, friends, or even romantic partners. How do you know you're with an energy vampire? YOU FEEL IT. You feel drained and exhausted, either while you're hanging out with them or after. This is particularly difficult for the more empathic types, as you'll have the tendency to feel drained more easily. Basically, energy vampires don't give you

that warm, fuzzy feeling inside. Instead, they have a vibration that is either too powerful or just completely out of range to yours. I'm sure you've noticed friends or family whom you feel comfortable or good around. This is because your vibrational range is similar to theirs. Energy vampires, on the other hand, feel like a succubus is stealing away your soul, and remaining around them can feel extremely detrimental at times.

2. **Eating nourishing foods to optimize your vibrational state.** This means limiting the processed junk (you know who you are, Tasty Cakes!) and incorporating more foods into your diet that are grown in their natural form. For example, raw vegetables tend to have a higher vibration than something like a Twinkie. Sad, but true. Always strive to reach for foods closest to their natural element; read the ingredients list (watching out for ingredients even your Harvard grad cousin can't pronounce) and try to eat foods that are in season. You are what you eat.

3. **Meditating using healing crystals or essential oils.** A lot of people don't "believe" in them, but understand that certain gemstones and crystals hold very high frequencies. Even pure-grade essential oils each contain a specific frequency. For example, something like Rose essential oil possesses a very high frequency. Just bear in mind that something containing a high vibrational state may not always be the best for you when you're feeling extremely fatigued or vulnerable. The energy within the gemstone, crystal, or essential oil may become too powerful with prolonged use and

can actually make you feel worse or a little out of it, so it's best to limit your exposure in these cases. Listen to your body. If you aren't feeling that great, don't hold a crystal for twenty-four hours or sit in a tub full of amethyst stones (ouch). It's best to use common sense here. For a great guide on crystals, I recommend *The Book of Stones: Who They Are and What They Teach* by Robert Simmons and Naisha Ahsian.

4. **Use sound therapy or Solfreggio frequencies.** I like to use something called binaural beats. Basically, these are audio recordings that contain a combination of simultaneous frequencies, which can have healing effects on our brains and bodies. They've been known to help with relaxation, focus, sleep, and in some studies, depression. If you're prone to seizures, please do NOT use these. If you don't want to use binaural beats, regular relaxing or meditative music (or in my case, electronic dance music) can really have some amazing effects on your body's vibration. You can use healing music or just your favorite song because it makes you feel good, and both would work. The key is to move toward whatever makes you feel good inside. There's also an arrangement of frequencies called the Solfreggio frequencies, which may promote physical and emotional health. These ancient tones were considered the "original" notes that the Gregorian Monks chanted in meditation practices and offer similar emotional effects.

5. **PEMF Mats.** This stands for Pulsed Electromagnetic Field Therapy Mat (say that ten times fast for fun). Basically, this is a mat you lay on, which is set to a

specific frequency to align with your body's, which can, in turn, help your body's cells regenerate. PEMF therapy has been used for years, speeding up the healing process for broken bones, helping inflammation and emotional issues, and more. I own one of these bad boys and lie on it for eight minutes a day. It's really an easy way to get you feeling back into balance with your body.

6. **Self-hypnosis.** This is another excellent way to start changing those subconscious thought patterns. In hypnosis, your body is in a completely relaxed state while your mind, still conscious, is vulnerable to specific affirmations or suggestions, which eventually can be embedded into your subconscious mind. Most of the time, hypnosis is not like what you see on TV, where someone starts barking like a dog or clucking like a chicken. It's something that must be repeated consistently, on a daily basis (like meditation), to obtain the full effect. There are thousands of self-hypnosis books, MP3 files, YouTube videos, etc. to choose from, and my advice would be to find one or two that resonate with you, one that's a comfortable length that works into your schedule, though I'd suggest no shorter than at least fifteen to twenty minutes so you can reach full relaxation. If it's too short, you won't give yourself the opportunity to slow your brainwaves down. You make time to eat breakfast, shower, and exercise, which is also self-care, so why wouldn't you make time to care for your brain?

7. **And the best way to keep your vibration high? DON'T STRESS ABOUT IT.** Forcing yourself

to "feel good" only makes you not feel good. Give yourself a little self-care, go play, dance in front of your mirror, get lost in thought, laugh, howl at the moon, or do whatever makes you feel good. The last thing you want to do is feel bad that you can't feel good. That's a recipe for disaster. Start creating more fun in your life, be sillier, don't care so much about every little thing, and realize that the more you can embrace the inner child in you, the more you're living from that place in your heart, maximizing your body's vibration.

Please note that none of the above techniques are replacements for regular medical advice. I am sharing purely what I know and have used to help with keeping my body's vibration at an optimal state. Also, these are more "quick-fix" type remedies, whereas keeping your body in a high vibrational state is more about how you're living day-to-day. It's about maintaining your emotional state, steering yourself in the direction of things that light you up and make you feel good, versus away from things that drown you or make you feel terrible about yourself. That's the simplest mechanism for living the high life: feeling like you're in alignment with the world.

Inspired Action

Let's talk about something called inspired action for a hot second. What is it? Basically, it's acting on something, but only when we feel called to do so. The difference between inspired action versus bending reality by the elbow, or putting it into a Hulk Hogan chokehold, is it feels good. It feels right.

You're doing it from a flow state, not out of desperation. Therefore, when you act from a flow state, you're automatically in alignment and on the path to your ideal reality.

Realize this: technically, there is no journey. You're already there. You act because it feels amazing, and you're inspired to act, not because you're trying to get anywhere. At the end of the day, where are we all going to, really? Our destination is often one of the imagination. The more we shift from a place of always needing to get somewhere or attain something, we realize that being happy now is really all there is. Everything else is a projection. Fake news. Everything you desire for your life comes down to one thing: feeling fulfilled in some way. So why wait? We always think that there's a world "out there," that the "truth is out there" (thank you, X-Files), and that in order to be fulfilled, we need to get "there." But is there really a "there," or is it our own little illusion? Whoa ... deep, man. I know. Think about it. What's stopping you from feeling good today? Is it this idea that you have to reach your destination first? Give yourself permission to feel good RIGHT NOW and see how your life shifts. Sometimes we don't realize how many possibilities are right in front of us until we stop pigeonholing our quest.

STEP #6

Embrace your uniqueness.
Give up attachments.

"Love yourself first and everything else falls into line.
You really have to love yourself to get anything done
in this world."
—Lucille Ball

The problem with trying to fit in is that you'll never fit in. Fit into what? Fit into where? Into a stereotype? Instead of the term "fitting in," let's replace it with "feeling accepted" because that's really what this is all about. Many of us have FOMO (fear of missing out) or FOR (fear of rejection). Normally, this stems from an early age. Maybe we were picked last for Pickleball in high school, or maybe our parents neglected us or didn't acknowledge us when we scored an "A" on a test. Instead, maybe we felt our family criticized us and only focused on that "C" we got in math class. Maybe mom and dad were too busy fighting with each other that they forgot your existence when you had just been bullied at school, or your friends ditched you after your boyfriend dumped you.

Whatever the reason (and there always is one), we don't necessarily like being the outcast. Even the loner who claims he loves being alone gets lonely and needs another human being to acknowledge him sometimes. It's because we are, that's right, HUMAN. Humans need other humans to function and survive. Sure, we can sit behind our computer screens and pretend that we're connected, but it's no substitute for human touch. And no, I don't mean human touch in some creepy "I'm going to poke you in the belly" like you're the Pillsbury doughboy or extend my long-ass pointer finger out at you like E.T. I mean touch in the form of a hug, a gentle touch of the hand, or even a handshake (as long as it isn't one of those metacarpal-crusher types).

We need human-to-human connection; however, that doesn't mean we lose our individuality in the process. We certainly don't need to take on other people's clutter, bad habits, or even identity. We can still follow our own path, so never act like someone's shadow because at the end of the day, the shadow disappears. It's like wearing someone else's shoes. They might be your size, but chances are that person's shoe formed a unique imprint to his or her foot (the arch might be worn, or the sides might be supinated); it just won't feel as comfortable as you breaking in your own new pair of shoes. It never is. Your foot will never be someone else's foot, just as your life will never be someone else's life. So stop pretending like your friend's shoe feels comfortable because you sure as hell know it doesn't.

Comparing Yourself to Others

The more you get away from comparing yourself to others, the better. Comparing only makes matters worse most of the time because it's driven strictly by ego. The little voice in our head says, "She has this. He's better than me. Look at her; I could never do that. She's much prettier, talented, and skilled than me." Screw that voice. It has no say in who you are and where you're going. It only holds you back from feeling good. It tells you that you're inferior. It tells you that not only is your cousin, relative, or friend over there more fun than you, but that he or she is prettier than you, smarter than you, richer, and more skilled than you, that you need to be like them. LIES. ALL LIES. Don't trust it.

That little voice attempts to sabotage your efforts. It loves remaining stuck in patterns, as it bases its "facts" on past experiences, memories, or traumas. It says, "My family has always been poor; therefore, I could never be like those rich people over there." It distances us from "those people over there" and creates unnecessary separation between us and "them" when really, there is no such thing as "us" or "them." I'll say it again. We're all the same stuff. I am no different than you, and you are no different than the billionaire you envy and put up on a pedestal. What separates you from him or her? Money? Fame? Fortune? What exactly does that mean? What does having more money mean to you? For someone who has always had money, it can mean very little, but to someone who grew up in poverty, it can feel like the answer to all of life's problems. But the billionaire might not agree with that. He still broke his leg in a skiing accident, lost his mother to cancer, found out his girlfriend was cheating on him, lost a lot of friends whom he found out were only after his money, and burned the roof of his mouth from Starbucks coffee that was too hot.

Sure, money helps pay the bills, it offers more freedom in our lives, but it can also lead us to greed, debt, or a lack of humanity if we're not careful. Money might mean control to you or solve a lot of things, but it doesn't make a person any more or less valuable. It doesn't make anyone any more or less of a human being. The only thing driving us to believe that we're separate is our ego and society. We've created this idea. The truth is, anyone has the potential to be rich; it's that most people don't believe that they can ever attain wealth for themselves. Do you think that every rich and famous person of today just fell into money? (Just look at Oprah.) Very few, maybe, but most believed they were better than what their ego or society told them. They made the conscious choice to succeed, and money wasn't necessarily their only end goal. They released the ego and the thoughts of feeling inferior or superior to anyone else. Instead, they focused on their WHY, their purpose and passion for living ... living from the heart and not their head. Whether it was a vision of a product or a service to others, they chose not to let others decide their future. They decided it themselves. **Remember: never let anyone dictate your life.**

This reminds me of an instance a few years ago when my grandmother visited the orthopedic doctor who had performed her partial hip replacement. My grandmother had undergone a great deal of suffering each day as, over the years, she developed a lot of degenerative arthritis around her right hip joint (to the point that whenever she stood or tried to walk, it resulted in a significant amount of pain.) She, being ninety-four or ninety-five years old at the time, walked out of the doctor's office that particular day, discouraged yet furious because the doctor basically told her to live with it and do nothing, that not even exercise or physical therapy would help because she was old. She took it as the doctor telling her to basically become bedridden (without him actually saying it to her face). I kind of got this impression as well. The doctor obviously was never blessed with bedside manner, and we all agreed that he didn't want to waste his time on a ninety-five-year-old granny, figuring she was going to croak soon anyway, so he wanted to get her out of his office as quickly as possible so he could move on to a more important patient. (This could be a whole other section about geriatric prejudice in society, but I won't get into that issue right now.)

Anyway, my grandmother decided that she wasn't going to let this "asshole" (in her own words) dictate her life, so she started physical therapy anyway, where she improved her strength, flexibility, and balance to the point where she felt less pain every single day. The moral of this story is to never let anyone tell you that you can't do something, no matter how massive it seems. Many times, the person is either so out of touch with reality or they don't care enough about you.

You Do You

Learning how to shut off those little voices in your head telling you to do something can be difficult, especially when they aren't your voices. They are the voices of everyone around you telling you how to act, what to eat, how to look, what to wear, what kind of job you need, and what kind of person you should be. These are the voices of your ego, your family, your friends, your significant other, and even your cat. Learning to do you isn't always easy. In fact, it's one of the most difficult tasks to cancel out everyone and everything around you. It's like trying to study in a crowded subway or watch television when the signal keeps going out. Your own voice gets drowned out by static or white noise. You might be on a whole different frequency than you think. A wise woman once said: **"Get out of your own head before it consumes you, bitch."**

Why can you feel fine one minute and anxious the next? Something happens that triggers a memory, which triggers anxiety. For example, you wake up feeling grounded, refreshed, and stable. You go about your normal morning routine as you would any other day. You shower, you pee, you brush your teeth, and you sit down to meditate for ten minutes. Suddenly, some random thought pops into your head about a work client. Something that "could" or "might" happen that would throw your entire day off (at least, you predict it will). You feel your heart rate speed up, your breathing becomes shallow, and your face starts feeling a little flushed. Now you're overwhelmed with this huge amount of panic, and it's making you feel like you want to crawl under a rock until the day passes. Where did this thinking come from? You tell yourself, "Dammit, I was so calm, looking forward to the day (sort of), and then these atrocious thoughts just started creeping all up in my grill. Now I feel like I can't escape from these thoughts. What the hell, maaan?" Blame your brain. Blame being human. As long as anxiety is not completely preventing you from living, it's completely normal for our brains to make every attempt possible to sabotage our positive intentions for the day. If anxiety IS preventing you from living (say, you are too fearful to even step outside), then there is something VERY deep-seated within you. It might be something that happened in your childhood, trauma, abuse, years of neglect, or it could be fluctuations in your hormone levels (that could be legit too).

Everyone experiences some sort of anxiety at some point in their life, but what would you do without it? Will you let it run its course throughout your body? Will you try to resist it? Will you numb it with pills or substances? Will you try to distract yourself long enough, hoping it'll go away on its own?

The choice is always up to you how you want to handle it. In his book, *Dare*, Barry McDonough states:

> *When you flow with your anxiety, the dark clouds quickly pass and are replaced by blue sky. If you do this right, you'll be surprised by how fast the anxious feelings and sensations change. But remember, don't look for that change or try to force it to happen. Allow it to happen in its own time. The paradox of healing anxiety is that you're attempting to generate a positive change while simultaneously being okay if that change doesn't happen right away.*

If you can manage to face it head-on, sometimes you'll realize that it's not such a big-ass monster after all. You are always in control of your choice of thoughts, whether you realize it or not. Even if it's your subconscious programming, it's still you, which brings me to this fact: if it's still you no matter how automated it seems, it still means that YOU can choose different or better thoughts. It still means that YOU have ultimate control over you. Your brain is NOT you. It's a part of you, sure, but you are so much more than just your brain. The brain is the computer, but YOU are the programmer. Nothing on the computer functions well if there isn't anyone to program it first. Your automated limiting beliefs are thus like a virus on the computer. If you don't do something about it, it'll rear its ugly head, take over, then decimate the hardware of the computer. I mean, you could always tell yourself otherwise. You could make up some freaky story about aliens hijacking your brain, but even then, that's the virus talking.

So think about this: Even when you feel completely out of control with your thoughts, how will you handle it? What will be your outlet? You can punch someone in the head, OR you can breathe, take a walk, or get away from the situation. You can either choose to remain inside your head all day, or you can choose not to and find something better to do with your time, like watching a cardinal pecking seeds out of the bird feeder outside.

We like playing a game of Battleship with our brains. We use it to help us make decisions and function on a daily basis; we tell it to do stuff, we know we need it, then we try to sink it. We talk down to it, tell it to "SHUT UP. GO AWAY. STOP TALKING." Essentially, this is the same as telling yourself that you suck. Even though you may not LOVE your brain or what it stands for, it's still a necessary part of you. The next time you find yourself overthinking, try telling your brain how much you love it, how you wish you could hug and squeeze it like a big gray squishy teddy bear, and that you're willing to compromise with it. Instead of going to WAR with it, embrace it.

Pamplemousse

We are followers. We see the latest trend, the latest product, the latest fad diet or workout program, and we want to do it too. In a year, we'll jump on the next bandwagon, but as long as something is popular NOW, we want in on the action too. Right now, I'm drinking a La Croix pamplemousse (grapefruit) flavored seltzer, and I'm enjoying it. I would never have initially purchased it if I hadn't first seen other people drinking it, however. In fact, I've never bought or liked seltzer water in my entire thirty-eight years of living. And God knows I never knew what the word "pamplemousse" meant. I must admit, though. I really like it. It's crisp, refreshing, and has no calories. It's the same with any product or service-based business. Hair salons, restaurants, nutritional supplements, you name it. Word of mouth referrals and online reviews spread like wildfire in the world of marketing, but what works for your friend Sally may not work for you. It does, at least, get you through the door to actually try out a product or service in the first place. Sure, you might try the pamplemousse, then decide that you really prefer the lime-flavored seltzer instead (true story). In fact, maybe you really hate seltzer all together. You dealt with it at first because it was the newest trend and you just HAD to try something you hated. You decided it tasted okay, but now you're tired and bored with the flavor. Like our taste buds change over time, so does life.

I remember the very first time I tried Indian food. I was in my mid-twenties, and my coworkers and I went to this Indian buffet nearby for lunch one day. I hated it. I gulped it down merely to be polite, but the flavors were just too exotic for my taste buds. It was too aromatic for me. I never had Indian food for years and years after that until my girlfriend asked if we could go out for Indian food for her birthday one year. I think I cringed a little bit; however, it being her birthday, I hesitantly agreed to the arrangement. And you know what? I totally liked it that time. Years had passed, perhaps my taste buds had matured, I broadened my horizons, and now I can honestly say that I crave Indian food pretty often now. Mind blown.

It's the same with our work life. We may start at a job we love or like, work at that job for years, and down the road discover that we feel bored or unfulfilled. Either it's the job that's changed (which these days is pretty common with the amount of turnover, layoffs, budget cuts, lack of incentive, etc.), or, on the flipside, WE have changed. Our priorities shift and what used to feel important to us no longer feels important. We value the balance between work life and personal life more than we used to. We want to find our purpose, feel fulfilled, and aren't feeling that way through our job anymore. Maybe our mindset has shifted gears from it all being all about the money to now valuing our free time and mental health. We evolve over time; that's just who we are by nature. The key is adjusting our outer environment to match our internal environment. If a mismatch remains, this is where things like depression, stress, anxiety, and hopelessness start settling in. Once we start feeling that nagging uncomfortable feeling within ourselves, we should pay attention to it. Many people ignore this feeling, but in reality, it's our higher selves reminding us of why we're here in the first place. It's the Universe telling us to open our eyes a little wider because this phase of our life might be coming to an end with a new phase just over the horizon.

Resistance Disrupts the Flow of Your Life (Detachment)

Recently, I cleaned out some of my closets and drawers stuffed with old clothes I never wear. I feel like it's a start to the process of letting go. It's hard to let go of old crap. I mean, I couldn't even bring myself to let go of some of the fifty-odd T-shirts I have on hand (it's amazing how many you accumulate over time) or some articles of clothing which I'm pretty sure I never wore a day in my life (probably because it was scrunched up into a little ball deep into the bowels of the bottom drawer). Yeah … never gonna wear it, but I'll keep it "just in case." Have you run into this issue? "I'll keep it JUST IN CASE." Just in case what, exactly? Just in case there's a huge brushfire that sweeps over my home into my sock and underwear drawers, eventually making its way into the other room, engulfing all BUT that one seven-dollar purple Hello Kitty T-shirt from Target that is three sizes too big on me? Is that really the only article of clothing that I'll be left with, and if so, how amazing that it survived! Or that pair of spandex gym pants that I've been saving all those years in anticipation that I might fit into them one day? Even though I never fit in them to begin with, but I bought them anyway to use as "motivation?" Yet here they sit in that bottom drawer, underneath all the comfy sweatpants that I wear for snow shoveling two or three times a year. I'm saving those too.

Our life works like a mirror. Like attracts like. I'm sure this isn't breaking news for you. However, this section is about attracting by detaching. Huh? How can I attract something into my life by not caring about it? Don't I have to think about something for it to come to fruition? You want the truth, the whole truth, and nothing but the truth? Well ... the truth is wishy-washy. Let me put it this way: if you desire, let's say, a new job, you direct all of your energy into wanting that new job, you think about it twenty-four seven, you can almost smell it, you can taste it, and you picture yourself, confident in your pristine black business suit, clutching your laptop, traveling the world, looking all important. You come to the realization that this MUST happen. You MUST have this new job, or else your world will crumble into a billion and two pieces. You do all the right things; however, the one thing you don't do is detach. There's a big difference between keeping your vibration high versus being attached to an outcome. Feeling good is a state of being, while attaching or obsessing over something is not only unhealthy, but it creates a state of resistance internally. Whenever you create polarity, nature will automatically want to balance itself.

In my years of studying Chinese medicine, I could see the connection between what ancient theories and today's quantum physics show us about our relationship to all things in nature. For example, yin and yang is the concept of everything being in balance in the Universe, which is the foundation of healing in Chinese medicine. When something is out of balance (i.e., too much yang creating a deficiency of yin or excess yin creating a deficiency of yang), emotional or physical problems arise. Let's pretend for a moment that you've been repressing your frustration for months. This could potentially cause an outburst of anger later on. Or say you're working all the time, putting your body under prolonged states of stress. This type of activity could eventually "burn out" the yang energy in your body, causing you to completely crash or physically and emotionally shut down. The emotional affects the physical, and the physical can affect the emotional. It all falls under the umbrella of returning to a state of energetic homeostasis. The aim of something like Chinese medicine and acupuncture is to regain this balance, which in turns reclaims our health.

If you recall, quantum physics shows us that we're all made of the same stuff as stars, planets, house plants, animals, rocks, and boogie boards. You're the perfect blend of dense organic matter, but also the perfect combination of energy, frequency, and vibration. It's the same reason we can become physically or emotionally ill when exposed to prolonged states of vibration in dissonance to our own. It goes for anything in the world. Too much of anything results in a deficiency of something else. I look at technology as a prime example. While modern technology is convenient, fast, and innovative, all of which are seen as positive, I often wonder about its long-term effects or the lack of face-to-face social engagement. I often wonder about the detrimental effects on our brains and society over time. Only time will tell, but I predict we're eventually headed in a direction of lack of human-to-human touch and interaction, which is essential to living.

So if all the energy is directed toward wanting to attain a particular person or thing, where do you think the deficiency lies? The answer is within ourselves. By wanting to attain something with such desire, we're actually telling the mirror, "I don't currently have this. I'm lacking in this particular area of my life." You're basically telling yourself that you feel imbalanced, not in equilibrium because if you were 100 percent balanced, you wouldn't have any desires or wants. Life would feel perfect for you. You would be whole and complete.

So you're wanting, wishing, desiring, and attaching to the object of your desire, and the more you try, the more the mirror image of yourself reflects back to you, saying, "I'm unhappy with my current life circumstances. I'm lacking." Like attracts like. What you give will be given back to you. What you try to take forcefully will be taken away from you. Simple physics—or is it?

It all goes back to living from a heart-centered space. The heart might not always want what the mind wants and vice versa. You need to be careful not to confuse the two. Think of it this way. The Universe doesn't understand positive from negative; it only understands in terms of energy and vibration. When we're happy and coming from a place of love, we send out a higher vibrational frequency, which is closer to our body's natural state (love). Whenever we think in terms of lack or feel emotions like fear, anxiety, anger, depression, sadness, guilt, etc., we're automatically lowering our body's vibrational frequency, creating more distance from the thing we want.

What does this say about the Universe's system of checks and balances? The moment we idolize someone or something, and the moment we do something out of manipulation for our own selfish benefit, is the moment we are misaligned. If we're attaching to someone or something, we're telling ourselves that we are on a lower frequency than it. The moment we remain neutral, the closer we are to that potential. You can still feel good, intend for things to happen in your life, and remain detached from the outcome. The key is to recognize that the Universe is here to take care of you. As long as you've asked, it's working in your favor. Don't worry about all the "hows" of your life, and trust. The issue is most people lose their trust because they give a time limit or try forcing their way through. That'll always backfire.

Realize that it's never selfish to want what you REALLY want.

"Mastering others is strength. Mastering yourself is true power."

—Lao Tzu

What do you want out of life? This is the age-old question. What do you want out of your life? Yes, YOU, not your significant other, not your parents, not Grandma or Grandpa, not your best friend, not Tony Robbins or Oprah or Dr. Phil or Wendy Williams, or even what Dr. Oz tells you. What's running through your heart? Yes, I said heart and not head because we have a tendency to live from our brain rather than our hearts. The heart is not just this weird beating organ inside our chest, keeping us alive and well. Did you know the electromagnetic energy field around the heart is sixty times more powerful than that of our brain? The HeartMath Institute discovered that our heart is an energetic powerhouse; therefore, we are not our brains. Sure, we're intelligent human beings, more intelligent than most species (note I didn't say all because we just never know what's *really* out there) because we have a higher consciousness. This higher consciousness connects to our emotions, and our emotions connect to our hearts.

This concept took me a number of years to figure out. You have books and motivational speakers talking about the power of our minds and thinking positively; however, only some authors or motivational speakers discuss in length about the heart and its connection to everything around us. Let's say for a second that you have a giant sunbeam sprouting out from your chest. It radiates around your entire body, and everything this beam touches, it infects with love. When you use this sunbeam in your favor, you can envelop the people, places, and things around you. Use this technique the next time you're with someone. It's sure-as-hell corny, but it works. Why? Because it reminds you that you have this magnificent electromagnetic energy field around you, and even though you can't see it, it still extends out to your surroundings. You control the strength of this beam of light through your emotion. The stronger the positive emotion, the stronger light you emit. Often, we cut off our beam to others whom we don't know, don't like, or don't trust. How do you know if your beam is emitting powerful light? You feel a heightened state of emotion. You feel warm and fuzzy inside, like someone just fed you fresh grapes and sprinkled you with magic unicorn glitter.

Think of it this way. Why do you think we're motivated by emotion? Why do we cry when someone close to us dies and not when it's a friend of a friend of a friend? Is it not just as sad? The difference is our relationship to someone. When we've created a heart-to-heart connection to someone close, as opposed to someone we might just "know" but have met only once, it's different. It's the same with animals and our pets. We become so close to our furry little friends, which make our hearts literally melt. I know I used to be able to sit and stare at my guinea pig Charlie eating his piggy pellets for a half hour straight, and I would feel the expansive fluster of butterflies fluttering around in my chest.

What Drives You?

Whenever you're wondering what forces are at play when it comes to your purpose in life, pay attention to when you feel in a flow state. How do you know when you're in the flow? You'll know. It's when your reality seems the same, looks the same, smells the same, the characters all appear the same, yet there's something a little different about it. Life just seems a little sweeter, a little easier, a little smoother, and people seem a little kinder and gentler. Money starts coming in a little easier, and you start really appreciating the little things in life. You start appreciating your own face in the mirror. Having an entire day "in the flow" feels completely amazing. For example, have you ever had one of those days where everything just clicked? Everything ran smoothly, the way the sun hit the clouds inspired you, the birds' singing sounded like a beautiful orchestra, and you noticed how the trees perfectly lined the street as if you were in the middle of a mesmerizing landscape painting. You stared at a rock and almost passed out because of its beauty. And you think to yourself, "I've heard these birds and I've seen these trees a million times, but for some reason, today I'm really noticing all of their intricate details, from the texture of the tree's bark to the color of the rock to the way the wind is creating a gentle sway in the tree limbs."

There's something cohesive about nature when you allow all of your senses to partake in its magnificence. Take these moments for what they truly are: you living in the moment. You aligning with the beauty of nature around you. You aligning with your source energy. This is home for you. It's these moments where all the nuances in your life don't matter in this specific moment. Take away all the clutter in your mind and all the attachments, and you're left with what? Pure bliss, contentment, and peace.

Feeling Good Versus Feeling Drained

Is it possible to remain in the flow indefinitely? Your next homework assignment (and I promise, it's not that terrible) is to pay attention to when you're feeling good versus when you're feeling drained. You'll know it because feeling good is this expansive lifting sensation that gives you energy, while feeling drained makes you feel like a dried-up boogery tissue that was just accidentally washed in with your jeans. You'll notice the difference when you're around certain people, places, or things. For example, how do you feel walking into your job each morning? Does it boost your energy, or do you feel like it's the end of the day before you've even arrived? How about your coworkers? Do they give you energy, or do you walk away wanting to take a nap? Your friends? Family? Relationship? If you break it down and think in terms of energy, go toward what brings you pleasure and move away from things that bring you pain or leave you exhausted. It's a simple formula that can provide massive results.

What Brings You Joy? It's All About the Heart and Mind Connection. Your Inner GPS System

What's one thing you do that brings you absolute joy? What's the thing that fills your heart, that thing where you lose track of time and space because you're so caught up in the moment that you forget that you were just craving French fries, forget about your family, your responsibilities, bathroom breaks, and sometimes even a shower? Left to your own devices, what would you do all day? For some people, it's playing video games, writing music, fixing things, or building things. For others, it's picking their nose, creating videos, scrapbooking, or playing with their pet rat. Maybe you haven't found that "thing" yet, and you're pretty bummed about it. Don't stress about it. Sometimes it can seem like an unending witch-hunt when we look for activities or people to make us happy. Why do you suppose most blind dates from online dating sites seldom result in a second date? It's because many people are trying to force their happiness. They're trying to rely on meeting someone who fulfills their number-one basic need, love. They're looking for someone to make them happy when, in fact, you can't MAKE anyone happy. It has to come from within. If you don't love yourself first and foremost and learn to date yourself, then most relationships with other people won't work out either. I, for one, always had the fear of missing out ingrained in me. Because I was unhappy with myself, I'd become extremely jealous seeing others happy and having a good time without me. I'd feel jealous and depressed at times, but in reality, I wasn't missing out on a damn thing. I just THOUGHT I was based on my perception of the situation. I could just as well have made my own plans, invited myself along, or took pleasure in having the time to myself. But I didn't want to be alone. Why? Because I fell victim to society telling me that sitting home alone on a Friday night while other people are out drinking at a bar made me a loser. In actuality, in my heart, I didn't even WANT to be at a bar drinking until ungodly hours of the night. I just THOUGHT I did because my brain told me, "Jen, you can't be a loser. You'll miss out on all the fun. No one sits home on a Friday night." See, what you THINK you want and what you really want can be VERY different things. For me, the challenge is always following my heart because we're constantly pressured by the forces that be. We have the ability to wake up from our hypnotized state as human beings and make a conscious decision not to partake in the external pressures of society, peers, family, and ego. We can remain neutral, ride the wave, and let things pass over us.

When there's disconnect between your mind and heart, you'll definitely feel some discomfort, either in the pit of your stomach or perhaps some constriction in the chest or throat. Over time, you'll be able to distinguish the differences with ease. We usually ignore these intuitive symptoms, or we never even notice them. With so many distractions, external forces, and modern technology, it's not that difficult to ignore, but if you can reach a point where you're listening to your body's own guidance system, you'll never steer wrong. Another thing that often gets in the way, other than outer distractions, is the ego, which we've gone over already in detail. We may think that we're listening to our body's clues when, in fact, it still might be the ego talking. How, then, can we distinguish ego from inner self? Pay attention to the INITIAL sign. The initial reaction by the body is, a majority of the time, your inner self and not your ego. It's that split second before the logical mind kicks in and tries to rationalize everything. If you become aware of the first thought or feeling that comes while making a decision, it'll almost always be right. After that, you'll notice the tides will shift, and you'll start having second thoughts about a situation, whether it be a job, a love interest, a car, food, or anything, pretty much. Your gut knows. You just have to listen to it more.

Confusing the Fear of Change with a Gut Feeling

Why are we so afraid of change? We're wired to plan out our lives, set everything up in a perfect order, and peg very specific actions or milestones on a very specific timeline. This isn't a terrible thing to do; however, if we don't follow it to a T, we freak out. We become attached to our little business plan so much that it stresses us out. We create a story in our heads that this is the ONLY way. We say, "I'm supposed to go to school, then graduate, then get a job (hopefully), then meet someone, then get married, then have babies, then maybe have a mid-life crisis, then decide to either go back to school or change my career, then get a divorce, then go find my purpose, then take care of mom in the nursing home, then sit on the couch eating peanuts and drinking wine until I die." We're stubborn, and we don't thrive on change. Why? Because it's difficult for our linear minds to be thrown for a loop. We consider it a threat to our previous business plan. Does it truly need to be a negative experience? Why do we make it seem like all change is bad?

Most of the time, it's coming from a place of fear. We fear failure. We even fear our own success. Even though we know that things can't be perfect 100 percent of the time and that we'll eventually make mistakes at some point along the way, it's still like one of those giant uncoated horse pills that's hard to digest. Sometimes, we even choke on it. Other times, we need someone to come give us the Heimlich. We know it's not our fate, yet we feel like it is. We know that there are abundant sources of income and a ton of ways to make money, yet right after we lose our job, we feel like it was the ONLY job that ever existed and that we might not ever work again. If someone dumps us, we feel like he or she was the last homo sapien on the planet. So how do we differentiate legitimate fear versus illegitimate fear? Is it possible that it's our intuition or a "gut feeling" telling us NOT to do something?

Legitimate fear is based on FEELING. As I mentioned above, this is that initial thought or feeling coming from the depths of our soul, saying, "Nuh uh ... not for you," while illegitimate fear usually comes across as a hopeless thought. It's when we tell ourselves, "You're not good enough for this. You're too inexperienced for that. You'll always be poor." A gut feeling usually acts like a lightning-fast impulse, while illegitimate fear tends to linger in our heads. For the most part, our intuition is spot-on, while our mind tends to have fluctuating results when it comes to change. Our mind often likes to dangle on the edge of our comfort zone, hanging on for its last shred of life.

So think about this the next time you're fearing something: is it because you truly believe that you'll lose your car, your house, and every penny to your name? Possibly. But chances are, you won't. Unless you were already living in a cardboard box with one dollar in your pants pocket, and a hurricane came by, and the only dollar to your name got so soaked while you were wading in floodwater that it basically dissolved in your pocket, you'll be okay. Even then, there's always a way out. If you tell yourself that there's no hope, then there's no hope. You're closed off to even a shred of possibility up your sleeve. On the other hand, if you give yourself the benefit of the doubt and know in your heart that the world will provide, maybe not in such a superficial sense where tens of thousands of dollars will miraculously float down from the heavens right onto your lap, but in other ways, it will. You might observe a gentle soul giving you the coat off his back, or a bakery owner donating his unsold biscuits to a shelter nearby. If you think and assume the world is full of bad people and bad things, then this will become your reality. If, on the other hand, you see light in the darkness, you'll start observing more positive things in your life. So, in essence, if the head says yes, you've got a fifty-fifty shot at it being right, but if the heart says yes, it's probably right.

What If My Inner Voice Is Silent? What If I Never Get the Call?

What is your inner calling telling you to do? Not sure? You ask yourself, "What if I have no passion or purpose, no inner voice telling me what I should do with my life?" First off, don't worry. I went through this for years, and it was basically a good way to give myself a migraine. Just because you can't hear your inner voice doesn't mean it's not there. Most of the time, we're so caught up in life's distractions that we have no idea how to really listen to ourselves. I'm not talking about the constant chatter in our brains that most of us have. I'm talking about something deeper.

"But Jen, how can I hear this inner voice if I've never heard it before and I don't know what it even sounds like?" That's a great question, actually. And you might be wondering if it's similar to trying to hear a dog whistle, something our ears are incapable of actually hearing. What is this "inner voice" I speak of?

Believe me. It's there. The best advice I can give you is to stop what you're doing. Just stop. Sit in a chair with your spine supported, or lie down and observe your breath. Focus on the clean air coming in through your nostrils with each inhale and the outward expansion of your belly, sinking back toward your spine. Focus on everything letting go: all of your muscles, your emotions, and your thoughts. And just focus on being there in the moment. Next, focus on feeling inside your body. Observe what you feel, whether it's tension, tingling, or another sensation in your limbs, or perhaps even the flow of energy (a sort of "buzzing") in the body. This is your body's energy, or "qi," and it is certainly real. Once you quiet your mind, relax your body, and spend time with yourself in silence, you'll begin noticing this voice pop up more often. And no, it's often not a regular audible voice saying things like, "Jen, start a business as an interior designer. You'll go far." It can come through as a subtle thought, a feeling, a slight nudge, or a knowing. Practice being with yourself, and don't try to force anything. Just let the thoughts exist. You can take it one step further by having a notepad nearby and writing whatever comes to mind afterward. It can be the tiniest thing or seem like pure nonsense in the moment, but still be significant later on. This is working with your innate intuition.

Flipping the Switch

We can easily flip to a different television station if we pick up the remote control, press a button, and voila! Channel changed. We do this by placing our attention and intention on changing to a different station. Intention essentially drives our action; however, if we were to only THINK about changing the channel, without acting, nothing would happen. In fact, we'd be stuck watching the same soap opera for hours on end, wanting to scratch out our eyeballs.

We can also flip to a different segment of reality, but only if we decide to shift to a different timeline. Does this mean we can simply flip our switch to a famous movie star or millionaire overnight? If what I'm saying is true, then wouldn't that be possible? Well, there's good news, and there's not-so-great news. The good news is that, yes, according to quantum physics, it is possible; HOWEVER, here's the kicker (and also the not-so-great news). In order to experience something in your physical reality, you need to believe it to be true first. So essentially, you need to believe that you're already a superstar or a millionaire before it's actually manifest. We know that it's easy to flip a television station because we KNOW for a fact that there's three hundred other channels existing at the same time. What's not so easy is believing something we've never seen or experienced before.

Let me ask you a question: do you believe that you have a million dollars? Do you believe with every ounce of your human flesh that you are famous? Most likely not. And if you do, you wouldn't be asking the questions above in the first place. You probably wouldn't even be reading this book. See, this is the part that makes it all not so simple. I'd say that if everyone had the choice, they'd surely accept becoming an overnight millionaire celebrity, but most people can't accept that they're actually worth it or believe it's even possible; therefore, nothing happens.

Days Off

How do you choose to spend your days off? Are you the productive type, spending the minute you wake up until the moment your head hits the pillow, crossing items off your to-do list? Is laundry, work, vacuuming, taking the trash out, mowing the lawn, and taking the kids to weekend soccer games your regular MO? How much time do you budget for yourself? Do you budget time for yourself at all? It's okay, you can be honest. Maybe time to yourself involves crashing out on the sofa, burying your head under a bunch of blankets so everyone leaves you the fuck alone. Is it always about others' time and not your own? Here's the fun part. It's okay to be selfish. Actually, it's not selfish at all to take care of yourself. So stop telling yourself otherwise.

What's selfish is not putting your self-care as a priority. What's selfish is running yourself into the ground so your body never has time to recover. What's selfish is you thinking you're selfish. Why do we spend our lives thinking that we need to always put others before ourselves? This is OUR life. Making time for yourself is one of the most important things you can do, and as long as your intent isn't to harm anyone else in the process, feeling guilty for getting a massage is NOT selfish. When was the last time you visited a library? There's something nice about the silence of a good old library. There's something oddly real about ... books. The smell of books, the feel of a good hardcover in your hands, the fulfillment with actually turning the pages of a good-smelling book, the mystery, the drama, the climax, the taste of a good book ... okay, well, maybe not the taste, but you catch my drift. There's something really wonderful about something non-techy. We all need time to de-scatter our flustered heads and reground, but the only way to do this is by handing ourselves a permission slip. Meditation, hypnosis, writing, or inspirational books can all become powerful tools in your arsenal, but you have to allow them into your world first.

"But I don't have time for me," you say. This becomes our biggest tall tale yet, and most of the time we believe it. We find time to check our Facebook in the morning, but we don't have five minutes to sit in silence? We have time to binge-watch the last four episodes of Stranger Things on Netflix, but we don't have twenty minutes to ground ourselves? We drive to work, but we don't have time to listen to an inspiring podcast or audiobook on the way? Instead of watching television for hours at night or reading the newspaper with lunch, why not sit and intently focus on what we're nourishing our bodies with? If we were to tally up the total amount of time we're distracted by social media, television, the latest gossip, checking personal email, picking lint off our shirt, and scrolling through our phones, we could have meditated, grounded ourselves, gone outside for fresh air, and set ourselves up for an awesome day, all in under ten to fifteen minutes. The other alternative is to get up ten or fifteen minutes earlier. We're talking fifteen minutes, not an entire day. Everyone has time. It's how we choose to utilize it; that's the difference.

Okay, So What's My Purpose?

People always used to ask me how I got into acupuncture, and I always told them the same story: "Wellll ... I had gone for acupuncture myself, and it helped me (half-truth), and I've always had an interest in health and nutrition and knew I didn't want to be a nurse ... umm, I had a couple friends in the field, asked about the schooling, and just decided to go for it. Part of it was also a career change for me. Yeah, I was stressed ..."

I know, lame. I wish I had one of those really dramatic stories about how I had one acupuncture needle stuck into my forehead, and it not only brought me out of a coma, but it allowed me to walk again, find the meaning of life, AND give up chocolate cake forever. But I didn't have some life-altering story.

Here's the REAL story. I hated my current job. I picked up one of those "What Color is Your Parachute" workbooks, took the tests, and Acupuncturist happened to be listed in my results for "which jobs fit my personality and interests." Yes, right next to Chiropractor, Physical Therapist, Horse Handler, Real Estate Agent, Spaceman, Grocery Store Clerk, President of the United States, etcetera. Okay, I am exaggerating on the last few, but my point is, I didn't know what the FUCK I wanted to do in life. All I knew was that I wanted to get out of my current job ASAP before I had another nervous breakdown. So yes, I had a book do the soul searching for me. That's the lazy person's way of doing it. So was the book right? Some parts of it were; it brought me closer to where I am now, but it was a little faulty. Were there parts about the job I liked? Absolutely. Were there parts I didn't like? Absolutely. Was I passionate about it? Honestly, no. Was I passionate about inspiring people to better their lives, give hope to people who won't give it to themselves, introduce people to new ways of healing themselves, and help balance their emotions? You betcha.

You don't have to always love what you do. It's why you do it. And it's often the stepping-stone to something better. In my case, I never loved sticking needles into old men's hairy butts or women's sweaty backs or faces or whatever. I didn't love learning every new technique or the latest and greatest acupuncture trick in the book, but I did and still do love empowering people.

You can be good at something, but that doesn't necessarily mean you're passionate about it. For example, I used to be great at filing and submitting medical manuscripts and scientific abstracts and posters sponsored by pharmaceutical companies to medical journals. In fact, I enjoyed doing it. Did it make my heart sing? Nope. So what's the difference between enjoying your work (or something else) and being passionate about it?

Your heart. Liking something and enjoying it come from the brain. Really, really, really liking something also comes from the brain; however, LOVING something comes from the heart. How do you know the difference? You know through feeling. If something causes you to feel expansive, like a bunch of fluttering butterflies are bursting out from your center, or if you feel like you just watched a Hallmark commercial, then you know. If something makes you happy but without that little extra "burst of somethin'," then it just makes you happy but not necessarily heart happy.

Just because you like something doesn't mean it's your calling. And just because you're not passionate about something doesn't mean you won't be in the future. I'm sure I could have just as easily been a chiropractor, physical therapist, or massage therapist if I put the time and effort into it, and I still would enjoy the same emotional components of the job over the physicality of it. I would enjoy talking to people, relating to them emotionally, and empowering them through words. The cracking, adjusting, stretching—even though I might have been competent at it—would be the means of letting me get through to people verbally.

It's okay if you haven't found something you're passionate about either. It doesn't have to be career related. Think back to what brought you joy as a child and start there. Even if you hate your job, are there any components of it that you DO like? For example, you can find the work you're doing dreadfully boring or meaningless, or your coworkers rather irritating, but maybe you really enjoy attending off-site seminars or "Lunch and Learns." (After all, who doesn't want free lunch?) Or maybe you hate staff meetings and feel like you receive no acknowledgment from your boss, but maybe you enjoy your job more when someone gives you positive feedback. Many times, we dislike our jobs because we feel unfulfilled, overworked, or underappreciated.

What would be more fulfilling for you? A different type of work within the same company? The same type of work but a different company? A different department with better coworkers? Or just something different altogether? It's okay to not know either. Knowing comes with time.

Your purpose doesn't have to be your job either. Let me clarify: YOUR PURPOSE DOES NOT HAVE TO BE YOUR JOB. This is where a lot of people get hung up. They feel like they just need to find a better job and BOOM! Life purpose checked off the list! I'm sorry to say it doesn't work like that. Purpose equates to meaning in your life. If you solely base your fulfillment and meaning on your job, then you're attaching to something outside of yourself. Sure, your mission could very well fall under your job, but the job itself isn't what brings you meaning. It's the satisfaction you feel on a deeper level, the emotion behind it, and the knowing that you're making the world a better place by you being in it. Don't confuse the ego's desire of appreciation from your heart's either. The ego loves the attention it gets from achieving a certain degree of status in this world, but the heart offers no judgment; its only mission is to keep you alive and fulfilled.

What brings tears to your eyes? And no, I don't mean chopping raw onions or watching the family dog get euthanized (been there, and it's literally one of the saddest moments in anyone's life). I'm talking about tears of joy. Yes, it may sound corny, but the tears of joy are a sure sign that you are on the right path and coming directly from your heart.

Release your grip, detach, and go find your inner cheerleader.

"The majority take the roads well-trodden but true success is achieved by the few who refuse to follow the rule 'do as I do' and independently tread their own path."
—Vadim Zeland

When I was in elementary school, my dad would always come watch my basketball games. Being that I was a tall girl for my age, taller than 99 percent of the boys in my class, naturally, I HAD to be good at basketball. I'd always dread after the games, though, because it consisted of my father critiquing my game and giving me pointers on how to improve. It was this constant focus on everything I did wrong in the game with one or two positive comments thrown in for good measure. Being an insecure and shy preteen, these little critiques after every game, for me, translated to, "You're not good enough." And over the years, I always battled with my self-esteem and really had to fight to gain back confidence in myself.

I often relied on other people's approval or acknowledgment from my friends and family to validate my abilities. It wasn't until years later that I realized the backwardness of this. The more we wait around for approval or acknowledgment, the more we realize we may never get it. Most people are too self-absorbed or waiting for their own validation to realize the impact positive recognition can have on someone's mood.

What does the word "underappreciated" mean to you? Do you need constant positive feedback to feel good about what you're doing? Do you rely on others to give you the inspiration? Or do you go and find it within yourself? See, if you're consistently waiting on other people to give you a thumb's up in life to keep you going, then maybe it's time to start rethinking your thinking. I'm not saying positive feedback isn't a wonderful way of keeping us motivated, and of course, it feels good. All I'm saying is that you shouldn't rely on it from other people. You should feel confident in your decisions, not feel confidence only when others approve. If something feels off while you're doing it, there's probably a reason for it. There's something about this job, relationship, or life decision that isn't jiving with your internal GPS. Sometimes it comes as a gut feeling, making you feel sad, depressed, or angry. These are all very real emotions telling you to re-evaluate things. Our bodies don't lie (not even our hips). So if you're looking for a gaggle of cheerleaders along the way, don't hold your breath. Hold your own pom-poms in the game of life.

Roadblocks

We all hit roadblocks in our life. Roadblocks are instances that throw a wrench in your steaming pile of optimism. You're jollily skipping along your yellow brick road, humming to yourself as you're starting to see fruitful things manifesting into your life, amazing circumstances and synchronicities, then BAM! Roadblock. You receive a phone call telling you a family member died. You're called to a meeting with the CEO, who tells you the company is implementing structural changes, which, unfortunately, don't include you. You get in a car accident on the way home that isn't your fault and total your newly leased Honda. You receive notice that your health insurance rate is doubling within the next two months, while your paycheck isn't. You hit a stop sign ... literally. Suddenly, you find yourself with a giant knot in the pit of your stomach, you lose your normally healthy appetite, and you wonder, "Why me? I lost my job that I loved, I lost the love of my life, my dog just died, and I've got a pimple the size and shape of Africa on my nose. What the hell do I do now?" You feel lost, confused, frustrated, a little depressed, and can't believe you have to start all over again. You've been working so hard, meditating every day, envisioning your dream life, thinking positive, eating better, and moving in the right direction, then THIS happens? What the hell, Universe?

The truth is one of two things: either you're still unaware of what you've been thinking about on a subconscious level (e.g., fear-based emotion), or you might actually be manifesting things that you think you don't want, but you actually want. Again, the Universe doesn't recognize good from bad, positive from negative. It doesn't speak your language; therefore, it doesn't acknowledge words such as "don't," "not," or "can't." (It's like that annoyingly accurate "don't think of a giant pink elephant" exercise where all you can think about is a giant pink elephant). Either what you're focusing on are the things that you "don't want" (e.g., "I don't want to work for this company"), which could very well translate to you landing a promotion and more hours at a job you despise, or you haven't really changed your subconscious beliefs. Words are just words, but if there's no emotion, or worse yet, negative emotion behind those words, nothing or the opposite may happen. What you think about, you bring about, and what you feel brings it into manifestation that much faster.

The other aspect of a roadblock could be that this particular situation is for your highest good. Remember, the Universe is always on your side. It likes to obey your commands when you really believe in something. So that seemingly horrible situation may be leading you down the right path to something better. We're human, after all, and of course, we always want instantaneous results and quick-fix solutions in thirty days or less. And oftentimes, the Universe gives us what we ask for, just not in the manner we often expect. Just because something horrible is happening now doesn't mean that it isn't leading us to something even better in the fastest way possible. Sometimes we do just need to trust the process.

The moment you release your grip on life is the moment you realize that when something happens to you, which seemingly steers you farther away from your "plan" in life (i.e., losing a job or significant other), it's actually the Universe rearranging things for your greatest good. This is the moment of awakening.

So many people lose their hope and vision once something happens that doesn't "fit in," something that we view as a negative occurrence. But what if we stopped to think that maybe this instance IS the Universe working in our favor; we just don't realize it because we can't see the big picture yet?

There are no true mysteries in life. Stuff happens for a reason, even if the reasons seem insane. Make the attempt to detach from a situation if it's dragging you down by the feet.

It may not seem like it's for your highest good right now, but later on you'll realize it probably was.

Resonance in Your Relationships

As you go through the process of making major changes in your life, you'll likely start to notice that not everyone agrees with them. You'll have friends or family who might get offended or feel like you're abandoning them in some way; you'll have friends who seem to drop off the face of the Earth, and you'll question your motives and if you're doing the right thing. Just remember this: the ego loves attaching to the reaction of other people and creating stories in your head. It wants to confirm any ounce of self-doubt or insecurity you've got left. These cluttered stories take precious space away from the new positive energy now entering your stream of thought.

Never feel bad for living in your new flow state. Other people's reactions will still be attaching to an older version of you, and that's okay. Let them. Realize that if someone demonstrates jealousy or demeans you for looking for more meaning in your life, it means that there's a vibrational disconnect. In this case, it's okay to limit yourself or release people who no longer resonate with you because you'll be making room for new people to enter your life: your soul tribe. This tribe consists of people who resonate with you on an energetic level. Sometimes, clearing clutter isn't only about letting go of "stuff." In some cases, it's about letting go of people who hold you down in some way.

Connect with others from a heart space, not a head space.

*"Everyone you meet knows something you don't know
but need to know. Learn from them."*
—Carl Jung

Sure, communication is key in life, and words have meaning, but the truth is a majority of human communication is nonverbal; therefore, it's important to become aware of how you're moving through this world. Most of us go about our days completely unaware of just how tense we really are or how many creepy looks we give others on a daily basis. It's only until we look in the mirror that we see our shoulders up to our ears and wonder where our neck went. We don't realize how much we give off death looks during the day, or how much eye contact we DON'T give others. When you sit across from someone, are your arms crossed? How about your wrists? Hands? Legs? Ankles? I doubt many of us are sporting "man spread" to other people. Not saying that you should do that (in fact, no one should adhere to man spread, as it's a disease in and of itself), but crossing limbs can be a sign of us shutting ourselves off from other people or the world. Do you always furrow your brow? Did I just make you try to furrow your brow to determine the answer to this question? Realize that this can be a sign of underlying anger and frustration. Do you give off the pathetic puppy vibe? I hate to tell you, but it's much cuter on puppies. Now, you might be asking yourself how any of this has to do with ANYTHING in this book, but on the contrary, I have my reasoning. Often, our chronic body language reflects how comfortable we're feeling in our life, how we're relating to others, and how open our hearts are. From an energetic perspective, crossing limbs can be a sign that we've closed off our heart from the world. So basically, body language says it all … or if not all, it says A LOT.

So how do you get to a point of total relaxation? How do you open your heart? First, start paying attention. It all goes back to getting to know yourself again and how you are communicating with your body. The interesting part about humans is that we mirror one another with our body language. The more we feel connected to someone, the more we mirror that person. Think, for example, of a first date. Two people sit at a table at some fancy restaurant somewhere. If both parties aren't chemically compatible, the woman will feel uncomfortable around her date. You'll most likely notice her crossing her arms or legs, which again signifies that she's closing her herself off from her date. She's basically sending the signal that her heart isn't willing to open up. On the other hand, you might notice that as the two become more comfortable with each other, their body language shifts, and things begin to open up. Legs become uncrossed. Bodies start to subtly lean in, eyes become locked, and they'll often mirror each other. They might even exhibit a little bit of man spread, which no one wants to see.

Experiment for yourself sometime. Eventually, the other person will mirror your body language in some aspect. Just be mindful that if you're in your head about it too much, it'll come across as not only fake, but mega creepy. Be subtle about it, be authentic about it, and really want to get to know the other person. Don't do it just because I told you to. Experiment with it because you want to form a deeper connection with another human being.

Humans and the Need to Relate (In Business or Personal Life)

Humans are always searching for connection. It's just in our nature. We want to relate to someone before we invite them into our circle. Take social media, for example. You won't click on one of those annoying sponsored ads that pepper your newsfeed unless you relate to it in some way. Think about what makes you relate to someone or something. Usually, it's because it's filling a void for you either emotionally or physically. It can be something to better yourself in some way, whether it's that you want to lose weight, become more mindful, declutter your life, become an author, help people, make more money, get rid of the bags under your eyes, increase your libido, boost your confidence, or boost your career. It all boils down to feeling good. Even if it's a coaching clinic about how to get even with your ex, it's still filling a void that makes you feel good (at least temporarily until the guilt and shame settle in) because you've been hurt emotionally. See, we all want to feel good, and it's our job to make sure that happens. It may require some effort, but the more we focus on feeling good in healthy ways, the more good things come into our world. I only give one warning: don't become confused with identifying with the ego rather than your authentic self. The more authentic you are, the more people will resonate with you.

Do things because you know it makes you a better person, not because you want something in return. Do things because you know that the positive energy you send out into the world is good for the Universe, even though you may not see people necessarily responding to your good nature right away. I guarantee this will happen eventually. You will and already have run into a lot of ungrateful people over the course of your life. You and I both know it. These folks who appear ungrateful, hateful, and obnoxious, however, are just distracted by life. When someone cuts you off on the highway without using their turn signal, instead of becoming infuriated at the white-haired dude in the forest-green Miata and wanting to flip him off, why not try to breathe, let go, and allow it to be what it is. Realize that the rage you feel inside will ALWAYS pass, chances are you'll never see this guy again, and becoming enraged is a waste of your time and energy. Imagine the other person's side of the story. For all you know, that man might have been rushing to the hospital or work; he might feel so stressed from his job or a personal breakup and so ungrounded that he barely has conscious control of what he's doing. (Sure, we'll go with that, just because it sounds better than the fact that the guy is probably an asshole).

Why would you waste your energy on an asshole who is too distracted to respect your space? The best thing you can do is remain neutral in these types of situations, send that person a peace offering, then let it go. Focus instead on the nice old lady who let you go in front of her at the grocery store line because you, too, were in a rush yesterday afternoon. Or focus on the other hundreds of people on the road who ARE abiding by the rules, driving the speed limit, using their turn signals, and driving politely. Why don't THEY get your time and attention? See my point here?

It's because we've trained our brains to focus on that one negative instance where that person's action brings up a strong emotion in us. We train ourselves to do this, as well as the media and external sources who have been training us since birth. Our negative emotions often become so intense, but if it's possible to feel so intensely in certain situations that make us feel bad, then it's completely possible to feel so strongly toward situations that make us feel good. And if it's possible to become so easily focused and pissed at complete strangers whom we'll never see again, then imagine how possible it is to focus on and love the people who don't piss us off every day. This is called gratitude. Joy. Love. It requires a bit of retraining to undo a lot of the negative thinking and emotions in a fear-based society, but when we start becoming aware of the negative patterns we're holding onto and work on shifting them, we reach a whole new level.

Believe it before you see it.

"The ego wants a full-blown strategic plan in ten
clearly defined steps to be accomplished in a week.
Yet without putting the ego on 'pause,' the soul's
magic can't happen."
—Penney Peirce

Did you ever have those days where everything seems to drag? You wake up exhausted, you go to work with your head in a fog, you feel a little insecure, a little antisocial, a little too slow, and you wonder, "What the hell?"

Congratulations, and welcome to the world of a low-vibe day. You wonder to yourself how yesterday you felt so high on life; everything came easily, you had abundant energy, you were friendly, motivated, inspired, and it was like you were skipping across fluffy clouds in your living room. But today you feel like shriveling up into a tiny fetus, pulling the sheets over your head and hibernating from the world. But how? And why?

Let's take a closer look, shall we? Did you sleep through the night? Did you go to bed late? Did you suck down half a bottle of wine before you went to bed? Was yesterday a stressful day? Did you get up this morning and rush around? Did you immediately go on your phone and check your email or turn on the news? Were you crazy busy yesterday and didn't take any time to yourself? Did you take too much time to yourself and lay around binging on Netflix all day? Did you skip exercise and instead ate crappy food? Have a big, fatty breakfast? Is your blood sugar taking a nosedive? Did you drink enough water?

If the cause isn't one of the above, then ask yourself, "Where's my head?" Are you being present with yourself, or are you living in the past or the future? Have you been worrying about things you can't control? Have you been trying to plan out every detail of your future, exhausting yourself in the process? Mental energy is DRAINING, so take a look at where your head space has been the past couple of days, months, or even years. Are you exhausting yourself by thinking way too damn much? This becomes that dreaded overthinking syndrome where you feel like you can't turn your brain off. No matter how many times you try pressing the "off" button, it's defective. Try this troubleshooting method: Instead of pressing the "off" button more aggressively, let go of it. Allow it to do its thing without getting too involved. Your brain is part of you, but it's NOT you.

Transition Period

As you're shifting to 2.0, you may enter the phase where you feel a little bit in limbo. Perhaps you're facing the big unknown. You may have quit or lost your job, found yourself single again, moved to a different location, and now you're wondering, "What the hell do I do next?" You might feel slightly lost, frustrated, uneasy, or resentful, even. The key ingredient here is to stay grounded and focus your energy on opportunity and advantages, not setbacks. You might feel like you're getting nowhere and wasting your time, or worse yet, feel desperate.

Let me tell you from experience: feeling desperate will get you nowhere FAST. Previously, when I had lost the "job of my dreams," I felt like I needed to get the first job I saw online ASAP. I'd sit and desperately scroll through my phone, clicking on all those too-good-to-be-true sponsored ads. You know the ones. They promise you a six-figure salary, full benefits package, a beautiful, luxurious work space overlooking the ocean, and an on-demand masseuse, but what they always seem to forget to include in the ad is the part about the SLAVE LABOR. I'm guessing this ad never attracted many prospects initially: *"Work seventy to eighty hours per week with one five-minute break to choke down lunch, hang out with miserable, obnoxious, smelly coworkers who push all their work off onto you; health benefits include a twenty-thousand dollar deductible; we won't pay you for weekends, but technically you'll still be expected to work, all included with a crappy, short two-hour commute; luxurious office view of downtown ghetto (hand gun included as a sign-on bonus)."*

Stop listening to others who imply that you're lacking in some way. Stick with your affirmations, meditations, your abundance, happiness, and self-worth YOUR way. If you wake up feeling a little down or pessimistic, recognize it for what it is, then go meditate or take a walk to clear your head (anything to prevent your brain from starting the downward progression to negativity neverland). Don't get caught up in it. Shortly after, you'll begin seeing more opportunities come into your life. You'll have a new appreciation for your unique abilities, strengths, and opportunities. Feeling afraid is a normal, healthy human response to change, but it doesn't have to prevent you from moving forward. Keep going, my friend.

Why Do We Question Ourselves?

It can feel like we're beating ourselves over the head with a bag full of quarters sometimes. Our subconscious minds have many years of training: Our parents tell us we should have done better, our teachers critique us, and our schoolmates criticize our abilities and appearance. We're endlessly bombarded by ads telling us that we need to look better, act better, make more money, upgrade our cars, eat the right foods, exercise more, and drink the Kool-Aid to feel better and more energetic. We're constantly faced with people, places, and things that promise us solutions to "be better," which basically implies that we're not good enough already.

What if we could just exist? What if we could walk around with a full-confidence shield strapped across our chests at all times? How would we react toward other people? I'd venture to guess that we'd accomplish much more for the mere fact that we wouldn't always NEED to accomplish what other people have accomplished. We'd no longer feel the need to compete. The only reason we don't feel like we're good enough is because we've had other people telling us this for our entire lives. Eventually, this sinks into our subconscious, and we believe it.

What if we could change these limiting beliefs? How would it change us? Would we live and act completely different? Would we have entirely different lives? What if you had no limitations on yourself? What would you do? Who would you be? How would you act? Who says you can't be happy? **You do.** Who says you can't be healthy, pain free, or attractive? **You do.** You think other people are telling you who you are, but when it comes down to it, you're the one telling yourself this story. You are the master and creator of your own life, but you're also the destroyer of your own life. People can tell you who to be or how to act, but it's ultimately your decision. How you react to others is your decision. You can take other people's words as truth, or you can find your own truth.

When Things Don't Go According to Plan

It was 4:30 p.m. on a warm, sunny Friday afternoon. I had just walked in the door after stopping for a bottle of Shiraz on my way home from work. I hung up my keys on the tiny little hook in the kitchen, brought my bags upstairs, slid off my shoes, then darted to the couch to relax and mindlessly scroll through my phone. Suddenly, I realized I had an unlisted-to voicemail from my company's CCO. Just to give you a little background, up until this point, I had worked with the law of attraction with spotty results. I'd always try imagining myself growing with this particular company. I'd envision more stability, more hours, a bigger patient load, and, naturally, more income. A couple months earlier, I received the announcement that the company was merging with a much larger parent company, which had multiple locations all over the country. I'd think to myself, "Okay, more growth, bigger company, equals more money and expansion of their holistic program, so this is good!"

I listened to the vague voicemail, then called the CCO back as soon as I could because, after all, my impatience wasn't willing to wait. How could I live through an entire weekend anticipating the news that the new company wanted to expand my hours? I had to refrain from uncorking that sexy bottle of wine and pouring myself a Jen-sized glass at least until after the call. I imagined spending my Friday night like a giddy teenager who just got asked out to prom, dancing around my living room, toasting to my mirror because my BIGGEST manifestation yet was coming to fruition! As the Macho Man Randy Savage would say, *"OHHH YEEEAAAHH."*

Then I called her back. And the news? It literally felt like my heart sunk into my stomach while my kidneys were simultaneously shooting up to my chest. Basically, what she laid out to me quickly over the phone (and I mean quickly, giving me barely enough time to process) was the EXACT OPPOSITE of what I was expecting. I couldn't believe the words that were coming out of this woman's mouth. Here's a summary: the company needed to cut costs and wanted to move the holistic program to a completely different setup with hours completely the OPPOSITE of what I had envisioned. She described it in such a way to sound less harsh, but I knew what it meant, and it sounded harsh. It meant the company didn't want to pay us any longer, and this was a way to still market the company as having a holistic presence yet wipe their hands clean of any financial responsibility. And work hours around the clinical schedule meant scattered hours on the outskirts of the typical nine-to-five. She told me to think it over that weekend, then she'd be in touch. Oh, I thought it over alright. I knew that wine wasn't going to be drunk that evening for celebratory reasons, but instead for a sort of grieving process, first being denial. Tears began streaming down my face. Suddenly, I felt a rush of hopelessness overwhelm me. I felt sick to my stomach. I didn't know where to go from there. Everything I had worked for, all my self-help and law of attraction readings, meditations, affirmations, crystal therapy, etc. … it all seemed to backfire … but why? I seriously told myself that this job WAS my purpose. Where did I go wrong?

Fast forward to now …

Sometimes the Universe works in mysterious ways. All I know is that it's always for our highest good. In my case, if the above never happened, I'd never have done the inner work I really needed to do, discovering that what I had spent years searching for was inside me all along. I discovered that my purpose was to share my story with the world through my writing and the content I create.

Sometimes in life, we need to be provided with experiences that lead us to our true passion. I used to think that working at this one company WAS my future. After all, I was making a decent amount of money, had awesome hours that left me with plenty of free time, I genuinely loved working there, the job, and all my coworkers, yet something better was still to come. You may think that where you are now is where you'll always be, but sometimes your higher self shows you that you deserve even better. You just need to listen. It might feel like the end of the road when, in fact, it's the beginning of a new and better path.

Have trust, be patient, and never forget that the Universe has your back. Your ideal reality is closer than you think. Just because you don't see results now, or just because what you see isn't what you imagined, doesn't mean that it's not right beyond the curtain. Things may be silently working in the background, just waiting to be unveiled. You can't enjoy a Broadway production without the behind-the-scenes crew. You can't witness a movie unfold before your eyes without it being written, directed, and filmed first. The same goes for your life. You are the artist painting on your blank landscape, but your painting begins with one or two colors, one stroke, then another stroke, then another, and another. You add a tree stem, then you add some branches to the tree, then perhaps some leaves, until it becomes a complete painting. It all takes time. The Universe doesn't give us a time frame. You only give yourself one.

Your Life Is Your Movie

In movies, we see a linear sequence of events happening smoothly from one minute to the next. But if you were to break it down, each movie reel is divided into segments, or freeze frames, of different scenes all tied together. If you happened to swap out one of the freeze frames, you'd find yourself with a different ending since one change can have a ripple effect on the entire reel. For example, if you replace one of the frames where a girl goes in for her first kiss with a boy she really likes to a girl being kissed by a boy who repulses her, you'd most likely find a different outcome of events thereafter than if she had kissed the boy of her dreams.

Think of your life like a movie script. Life is divided into segments, or scenes, which we have the ability to change at any given point. This can then yield different outcomes. Here's an interesting question. If we can work these segments of our lives in any direction, can we determine the outcome before it's even happened? And if so, how? Since life also happens in frames, the only thing that tells us that to achieve a specific outcome (e.g., C), you must first do A + B is our linear thinking. Our brains are seemingly not equipped to handle the concept of everything happening all at once. In fact, it seems like such a ridiculous idea; however, if we focus on a potential outcome in our lives and forget the "hows" (how we get there), pushing aside linear thinking for a moment, then we can achieve the same results even faster.

The idea here is that experiencing an outcome as if it's already happened and truly having the brain believe and trust in whatever we want allows us to master our minds. We've managed to override the ingrained limiting belief systems AND our ego. The difficult part for most people is getting past the "I'll believe it when I see it" mentality and instead telling ourselves, "I'll see it when I believe it." If you set the intention to experience an event before it's actually happened, you'll see it or some form of it in due time in your physical reality. It's not some form of magic voodoo or witchcraft, either. It's about making a decision. It's not about waiting to see if it will or won't happen. Instead, it's a knowing. Again, it all goes back to the quantum field where any and all possibilities exist for you. Think of each movie scene like a chess piece. With each segment, you have the ability to choose which direction to go, which move to make. Your reality is divided into segments, so each choice you make affects your future outcome.

Importance of Having Presence

Years ago, my Uncle Dominic drowned when his car ran off the edge of a small cliff into the river at one of the nearby parks early one Friday morning. Morbid thought to go with your morning coffee, I know. He was a school crossing guard in the neighborhood but never showed up for work that afternoon. Someone had discovered a car almost completely submerged into the Raritan River, and Dominic happened to be inside that car. Apparently, he had taken a curve along the dirt road a little too fast, or so we assumed, and ran his car off the cliff.

My family received the phone call later that afternoon. In a way, no one in my family was completely shocked. After all, my uncle, a functioning alcoholic, would often drink in his car (my family could never think of what to buy him for holidays and always enabled his addiction by buying him one or two of those really large jugs of red wine). I remember at Christmas his eyes would light up as he tore away at the cheesy snowflake wrapping paper, revealing a heavy, bulbous jug of Italian Merlot glaring back at him. This was his world. We had just assumed Dom had been drinking the same morning that he died. Whether he was or not, we'll never really know. Seeing his lifeless body hanging on life support in the hospital that afternoon, I observed scrape marks extending the length of his arms which, to me, meant that he struggled underwater before he went unconscious. It was my grandfather's decision to pull the plug, and I remember watching Dominic take his last breath, his brain already dead. He took a few deep breaths on his own after that, then it was all over. The rise and fall of his chest stopped. We all grew silent, said our goodbyes, my grandfather kissed Dominic on his forehead, and then we left.

Death is a strange thing. It never fails to give us a different perspective on life for a few moments. That weekend, I couldn't get the image out of my head of my uncle trapped in his car underwater. I imagined him opening his eyes, disoriented as to what exactly happened, only to realize that he was underwater yet could still breath because the windows of the car were sealed. I pictured him panicking, knowing that it would only be a matter of time before the air ran out or the water began pouring in. I could see him pounding his fists on the windows like there was someone out there to save him, but the pressure of the water made it impossible to escape. He was trapped, just him and his thoughts. He wasn't far away from civilization. It was a public park. Would someone discover him before time ran out? Would he be rescued by some brave jogger who happened to be in the park that same morning or perhaps by a police officer riding through? Would he see God? Angels? Or his sister, Clara, who had passed away many years earlier?

It's not until we're faced with death that our life matters. We live distracted in our heads, working, buying material possessions that make us feel good temporarily, then spend our time chasing or searching for the next best thing to fulfill us, yet whenever we attend a funeral or wake, we're different people that day. When we visit our father in the hospital who just suffered a heart attack, or we find out our sister has stage four breast cancer, we live a little kinder, gentler, and with a little more compassion. Then tomorrow comes, and the next day, and we revert back to our old, distracted selves. Why does it take moments like these to change our perspective? Why do we wait until someone near and dear to us passes away to feel grateful and be compassionate toward others? Think about it. If we live from a place of compassion and gratitude, our lives would drastically change. We begin discovering more about ourselves than we ever imagined. Things that once seemed important suddenly lose their luster.

In my uncle's case, he was a lonely man. He lived his life carefree, he seemed jolly and happy, and we let him be that way, but by understanding and feeling compassion for my uncle, we'd see that he needed more love and inclusion in his life. For him, he found comfort and love in the form of alcohol. If my family and I took the time to understand him more, we'd see a lonely man, sitting at his desk chair in nothing but his underwear in his dark one-room apartment in the nearby Somerset Hotel, listening to his police scanner before his eight o'clock bedtime. No television, no friends, and no family with him. Just him, a jug of wine sitting on the floor next to him, and his police scanner.

Discover the power of inner work. Nourish your inner child.

"Some day you will be old enough to start reading
fairy tales again."
—C. S. Lewis

"**P**ete" came into detox one day. He had already been through my detox center less than six months prior, but he mentioned how he had screwed up and relapsed, so he was back for another week. His two-year-old daughter had recently passed away from leukemia, and opiates were his only coping mechanism. I could see his eyes well up with tears as he spoke to me about his daughter. He had plans to go away to a thirty-day rehab facility, maybe even a ninety-day one, not so much for his addiction but to get away for a little while. He wanted to separate himself from his home life. I treated Pete a day or so into his arrival with acupuncture. After the treatment, he said that he cried a little onto the massage table headrest.

"Men aren't supposed to cry," he said. He fought back more tears.

"Of course they do," I responded. "You need to cry. You need to let out whatever's eating you inside. We're all human and need to let it out of us." I felt such compassion for Pete as he thanked me with a slight smile out of the corner of his mouth and then left the treatment room.

I thought about him the rest of that day, how horrible it must feel to lose a child so young and relapse on top of it all because you don't know any other way to cope. Pete did end up going to a thirty-day rehab after his short stent at detox. I remember I wished him well as he waited for one of the technicians to gather up his luggage.

When I see an addict, I see a human being who is being tormented by their own demons. This demon could rise in the form of a past or current trauma or a lifetime of feeling unworthy and unaccepted. We all want to feel good. We all want to feel accepted. We all want to feel loved. We all want a perfect life. Sure, we'll face difficult times, losses, trauma, and sadness. But how will we deal with those demons? Will we internalize them? Or will we expose ourselves and release our feelings? The more we internalize, the more builds up inside of us. The more emotions we hide, the more imbalanced we become. Sadness can turn into chronic depression. Frustration can lead to hateful outbursts. Worry can cause chronic anxiety. The more we internalize these feelings, the more we add fuel to these toxic emotions. It's akin to a pressure cooker. If you keep letting the pressure build up without an outlet for the steam, eventually the pressure will be so great that it'll result in a violent outburst: the cooker will explode, the lid will blow off, and your nicely cooked meal will be splattered all over the walls, possibly taking out anything and everything in its path. We're the same way. If we don't find a healthy outlet for our emotions, we'll blow our lid. We'll end up with a violent outburst directed at someone else or ourselves.

Releasing emotions is crucial to change and progression, but we need to do so in a healthy way. We can try to numb our feelings with booze or illegal (or legal) substances. We can numb ourselves with a pound of chocolate, a gallon of ice cream, sex, porn, gambling, or shopping, but the truth always remains inside. These are temporary fixes that can result in long-term damage. Suddenly, we dig ourselves a gaping hole, and we struggle. The more we hold inside, the more it eats away at us.

According to traditional Chinese medicine, the accumulation of stress and frustration leads to stagnation in the body, which begins the disease process. So that constant nagging stress that's been slowly building up inside? Suddenly, you start developing physical symptoms. You start feeling distention in the chest, you start experiencing headaches every day, you get fatigued more often, and your thinking becomes foggy. When any emotion is held for long periods of time in the body, it begins affecting the energetic components of our organs. Even too much joy can harm us (think of someone who is bipolar in his or her manic stage). Nature always wants to be in balance, and part of that balance is finding healthy alternatives to release the negative emotions.

Your Inner Child Is Waiting

I remember camping out in my backyard as a kid. My father would set up this blue tent large enough for him, my brother, and me to all sleep in. I'd drag out the thick dark-red silky sleeping bags from the cellar and line them up perfectly in straight lines inside the tent. My mother would stay inside and get the house to herself for the night while my brother and I would sit in the tent eating Oreos, drinking cold milk, and telling each other stories about witches and ghosts. How could something so simple like sleeping out in the backyard literally fifty feet from the house bring me so much joy? I still remember the plastic smell of the tent lining. There was something about it I loved. Maybe it was the fact that I got to eat Oreos late at night without brushing my teeth afterward, or maybe it was fun for me to be with my dad and brother, being stupid silly all night.

Sometimes we don't realize it, but the smallest things can nourish our inner child and put us in a state of ultimate joy. We don't necessarily need to travel on a big fancy expensive vacation to some exotic island or do some spiritual soul searching in a desert in the middle of nowhere. Sometimes what we need is literally right in our backyard. The key is opening yourself up to trying something new, even if it's as simple as drinking your morning coffee outside instead of inside or going to a 4-H Fair and petting the alpacas one Saturday afternoon (or better yet, visiting an alpaca farm. One word: AMAZING). You can read a good book in your lounge chair or write a short fictional story at your local library. It doesn't need to be extravagant. Start small and learn how to do things for yourself. The difference is doing things that ACTUALLY make you happy, as opposed to doing things that make other people THINK you're happy. Life isn't happening to you. You are creating it. Stop being a victim to life and take control of your joy. You don't need to find joy where others do. A majority of the time, it shouldn't even cost you a dime.

Learning to Love Yourself Again (Nourishing the Spirit)

For a long time, I hated myself. Not every single day, but on days where I felt I was too chubby, not smart enough, or days where I constantly compared myself to others. Self-loathing is one of the worst things you can do. It leads you down this dark corner of the soul, almost like a hidden dungeon deep within the layers of yourself. It becomes this perpetual cycle of never escaping, otherwise known as the "land of stuck." It begins in the mind, then over time, it slowly but consistently swallows up the rest of your body. Sound like a bad horror flick? Maybe, but this is life, and sometimes life acts like an awful B-grade slasher film, dumb blondes and all. You get sucked in, realize you can leave at any time, and yet you choose to suffer your way until the end.

The best thing you can ever do for yourself is learn how to love yourself again. "But Jen, I don't think I've ever loved myself," you might say. Here's my answer to that: NONSENSE. The minute you were born, you loved yourself; you had no qualms about yourself or others. You didn't self-medicate or find yourself in bad relationships. You didn't fill the void with food or new shoes. You didn't look in the mirror and curse God. You only knew how to be you in your truest form. Here's some good news: you're still you. The minute you start learning how to communicate with others, listen to others, and serve others, you start the negative self-talk. This begins the process of leading you away from yourself and closer to that B-grade slasher-flick life.

Another important strategy is detaching from the "I'm weird" mentality. Just because someone can't relate to you or your story doesn't automatically make you weird. You just haven't met the hundreds of thousands of other strangers going through exactly what you're going through right now. No two people are identical, but there will always be someone you can relate to; that's almost guaranteed. Most women in particular are not up-front about their insecurities because they feel "weird" too. See? That's already one thing you have in common with someone else. Many people are embarrassed, ashamed, and self-loathe for this very reason. They feel like the outcast.

The more we turn our focus away from what we hate about ourselves, the more we create space for what we love about ourselves, and the more we nourish our spirit. Sure, you nourish your body from time to time with dirt-flavored green tea smoothies, and you even nourish your mind periodically with romantic comedies or self-help books, but how often do you nourish your spirit? What exactly is spirit anyway? To some people, spirit sounds like some ominous, dark, shadowy thing lingering in graveyards or creaky hundred-year-old houses. To others, it sounds like a religious thing, but essentially, spirit is you. Your mind, also known as "Shen," is spirit. You can understand how connected a person is to his or her spirit by looking into their eyes. The eyes are known as the "windows to the soul," which is why someone who "isn't right in the head" may exhibit cloudy or vacant eyes. By nourishing your spirit, you take yourself out of your left logical brain and deeper into what makes you thrive, what motivates you in life, and your true authentic self.

Without sounding too overwhelming, here are a few ways to practice nourishing your spirit and your Shen. Maybe you do some of them already. Fantastic! Keep going and maybe try to add at least one more to your repertoire. (Don't worry. These are pretty basic.)

1. **Meditate.** Begin with five minutes every morning as soon as you get up. (Yes, you can use the utilities and wash your eye crust first). But I recommend you meditate before you turn on your cell phone. This is

a must. Meditation can consist of closing your eyes and just letting the thoughts flow in and out of you. Try to feel into your body (really feel it). See if you can feel tingling, warmth, or an expansive sensation anywhere in particular, beginning with the soles of your feet, traveling all the way up to your heart and limbs. If you "don't do meditation," do it anyway. Sit in silence. If you're into crystals and gemstones, or essential oils, these can definitely aid the process, too, but not required.

2. **Listen to Affirmations.** Regular or subliminal affirmations work, your choice (subliminal affirmations are hidden in music to bypass the conscious mind). You can find a lot of free stuff on YouTube, or you can find some pretty cool MP3s to download. (I do have some subliminal affirmations up on my website and YouTube channel both for free or a small fee if you want something easy.)

3. **Listen to Music.** This one can't get any easier. Raise your vibration with uplifting music. Just make sure it's not death metal or gangsta rap (unless it's the uplifting kind). Buy yourself a decent pair of headphones and listen to music that makes your body want to move. For me, it's dance music or electronic music with heavy beats and inspirational lyrics that often results in me crying (in the good kind of way). This is one of the fastest ways to raise your vibration, and it's also an amazing way to release any kind of stuck or repressed emotions.

4. **Dance or Sing.** Let's get you out of your comfort zone a little bit on this one. Ever hear the saying,

"Dance like there's no one watching"? Well, it's true. So grab that hairbrush and use it. You can even whip out the vacuum cleaner and use dancing as a strategy to get some housecleaning accomplished. (For the more shy ones, you can close your eyes and dance in your head for a similar effect.)

5. **Keep a Dream Log.** Jot down your dreams (if you remember them). Write whatever comes to mind when you first wake up. I'd recommend writing with a pen or pencil as opposed to tapping it into your "notes" section on your phone. There's something about doing it old-school for releasing subconscious lingering "stuff." In fact, I still write in cursive, if that's still a thing these days. (I also still buy CDs, and I'd still probably buy cassette and VHS tapes if I could *child of the '80s raising hand*.)

6. **Keep a Gratitude Journal.** Write every morning or every night before bed whatever thoughts are flowing in or out. Keep a gratitude journal and list ten things you're grateful for each day. These can be anything from your morning cup of coffee to having fluffy warm socks on your feet. Focus on one thing at a time, and really try to feel your heart center get as warm and fuzzy as your socks. Don't force it. Just allow yourself to feel what's there. The less overwhelmed you feel doing little daily rituals such as this, the more beneficial.

7. **Automatic Writing.** Writing is a form of meditation and can be extremely therapeutic. It's a great way of expressing things inside that you'd probably never say and allows you to dig deep into your subconscious

mind. It pulls out all the things that might be too uncomfortable or embarrassing to admit. Sometimes when I feel upset, I write it all out. Sometimes when I feel really happy and grateful, I write it out. And sometimes when I feel nothing, I force myself to write, and suddenly, words start flowing out of me. You just need to begin. It's like life. Just do SOMETHING, and the rest is history.

8. **Write Yourself a Love Letter.** Okay, you can stop rolling your eyes at me. Yes, I'm not kidding. It may help. You've spent so much of your life seeking love and approval from other people, so why the hell can't you send yourself some love for a change? No, it's not stupid. No, it's not egotistical or narcissistic. You need to remind yourself of your beauty inside and out. So go ahead. Write yourself a love letter. This could be as quick and simple or as complex as you want to make it. Just do it. Write it out, even if you don't yet believe what you're saying. Eventually, you will. After you write your letter, speak it out loud to yourself. Do this every single morning and every night. I don't care if your boyfriend, your husband, or your girlfriend laughs at you. They laugh because they probably wish they had the guts to do it too.

You deserve love. You deserve a love letter. You deserve to see and hear it with your own eyes and ears and feel it in your heart. I remember when I wrote my first love letter to myself the summer of 2018. I really dug deep into the parts of myself that were feeling insecure. It seemed really dumb to write at first, writing statements that seemed at first fake;

however, when I read it out loud to myself, I started bawling my eyes out. I felt such emotional ties to what I was hearing—it was like all of this "stuff" that I was withholding from myself came out. It was exactly what I needed to hear, and I remember I could barely get through the entire thing. My voice crackled and shook like a little girl who just found out her hamster died. I needed the emotional release, and my stuck feelings eventually turned into bouts of inspiration.

9. **Go on Dates with Yourself.** Sure, if you're involved with someone already, then by all means go on dates with them, too, but it's so important to learn how to date yourself. Why? So that you can remind yourself that you love yourself so you aren't constantly relying on love from other people. Learn to be comfortable with yourself fully. Plus, it's fun. Go outside your comfort zone a bit. I know this element was extremely difficult for me, as shifting out of where I felt comfortable was equivalent to being thrown into the deep end of the pool when I very well knew that I couldn't swim. It's THAT feeling.

All I'm asking for is at least five minutes each morning. If you can go longer, go for ten. You can do anything for five minutes. Fight the impulse to check your devices first thing (which have the tendency to make you feel grumpier and fog-headed). Replace the phone-checking with a positive behavior. You might find that your impulse goes away completely and realize how good it feels to wake up and actually feel IN your body. This will absolutely jump start your day.

Stop Pretending to Meditate

But wait. Didn't I just tell you to meditate? Sounds contradictory to most of what I've said so far, doesn't it? Not that meditating is bad because it's not. However, if you're meditating day after day and nothing in your life is changing, then it might be time to take a step back and not try so hard. Stop chasing after life. Stop chasing after desires, and you know what? The moment you let go of the desired outcome and you start actually living your life, the more you'll shift your life. If you're trying to make something happen to you or for you, you're in the wrong mindset. Once you project something for the future, it'll always be in the future instead of identifying with it NOW. It's better to have five solid minutes of a good heartfelt meditation than a two-hour one. So if you really feel like one of the above exercises is not resonating with you, don't force it. Forcing only causes more resistance within you. Instead, try something out and see what resonates. Do you like writing more than sitting and meditating? Okay, there's your answer. Do you enjoy passive activities like listening to music more than dancing? Do you find your mind wandering when you're either writing or listening to affirmations as opposed to just listening to music? Pay attention to the clues your body is giving you.

Your Morning Routine

Your morning routine can be the difference between you living as a superhero or you living as a frazzled mess. The importance of setting a good morning routine is often underrated. Think for a second. What does your morning look like on a daily basis? Do you rush out the door, or are you one of those people who needs a solid two to three hours in the morning to set the tone? How do you feel when you wake up? How do you feel as you leave your house? We're going to break your morning routine down a little further here, and I'm going to give you a quick exercise.

Take out a piece of paper and list three columns: MIND, BODY, SPIRIT. Now, I'd like you to list ALL your morning activities which nourish your mind, body, or spirit and place each in a column. For example, your MIND column might include activities like reading, writing, affirmations/ mantras, visualization techniques, or goal setting; your BODY column might include exercise, nutrition, breathing exercises, hydration, sleep, or showering/hygiene; and your SPIRIT column may include things like meditation, any type of self-care, nature, reiki, music, laughter, etc. You catch my drift. List EVERYTHING you do in the morning. And then, I'd like you to create a fourth column and title it "Activities that do NOT contribute to the MIND, BODY, SPIRIT." List any and all activities that didn't fall under those initial columns. For example, this could be something like social media, television, eating potato chips for breakfast, etc. Basically, this column includes any activity that is not NOURISHING for your mind, body, and spirit.

Once you've completed this list, take a look and see how balanced it is. Are most of your morning activities falling under only one category? Did you find that your fourth list is way longer than your MIND, BODY, and SPIRIT lists? See what you're currently doing and if you can add any activities. The goal here is to choose at least ONE activity for each category and implement these into your morning routine. Having a balance of all three nourishing categories not only leaves you grounded but will set you up for an amazing day.

Add value to others. You always have a message to share, whether you know it or not.

"Make the world a better place because you have lived in it."
—Edgar Cayce

I used to fear public speaking. On the surface I appeared cool, calm, and collected, but I was secretly dying inside. Whenever I had to give a speech to an audience, I'd practically pass out from the anxiety beforehand. Even little ice-breaker drills in class would freak me out (when you have to simply raise your hand, say your name, and where you're from). I'd start clamming up, my face would flush like an alcoholic Santa Claus, my palms would sweat like a teenage boy around his twenty-two-year-old teacher, and my heart would start racing to the point where I could feel my entire heart pounding through my chest. I'd start getting lightheaded and queasy, my stomach would knot, and I'd have to write out my entire speech beforehand word for word (a security blanket for myself because I had a huge fear of losing my train of thought or having a complete mental block). I'd strategically place my script directly in front of me, making sure I'd look up and make eye contact enough times to give off the appearance that I was speaking all from memory. This was my method, and it seemed to work. I actually don't know how some people do it. They speak for hours with nothing more than a note card or bullet points up on a PowerPoint. I've gotten better with speaking in public, however, and I find that the more I speak from my heart, the easier it is. I think I'm much better off speaking one-on-one. For me, I can relate to someone individually without feeling judged or critiqued.

My point is that writing always felt like the right outlet for me to share my story or to give back to others without the added pressure. Maybe I don't have some huge, sad, fascinating tale to tell, but maybe it'll strike a chord with someone, and maybe that someone will change his or her outlook for just one day. One day is just enough time to shift something in someone to potentially make life better in some way. I suppose that's my intention here. Writing is therapeutic in its own unique sense. You don't really know what's going to come out of your head until the pen hits the paper (or the fingers strike the keyboard).

Realize that we're all messengers at heart. We're always delivering a story, whether we realize it or not. We're always sharing our knowledge with others. If you think of your day-to-day, consider how many times you give advice to someone, offer your opinion, or speak about something you're passionate about.

Everyone has a message to share. We all have a story. The question is, what will you do with your story? Will you keep it hidden for fear of looking awkward or vulnerable, or move beyond your ego and share it, thereby helping someone?

Our Best Moments and Breakthroughs are Often in Our Darkest Times

I find that in our darkest moments is where we pull the best stories out of ourselves. It's in those days when we feel the shittiest that we can help someone the most. Why? Because in our darkest times, we are the most vulnerable, and it's through our vulnerability that we are truly ourselves. We become compassionate, and people relate to and feel that compassion within us. When we feel vulnerable, we forget to hide behind the mask of our egos and truly show up. Other people take comfort in seeing other people uncomfortable sometimes. Why do you think that is? Not because we truly want to watch others suffer, but because seeing others vulnerable makes us feel not so alone. It reminds people that other humans go through it too. There is great comfort in that.

Our lowest points can also be a time of our greatest breakthroughs. When we stop forcing our way and surrender to the flow of life, then ideas, insights, and revelations suddenly come to fruition. Something inspires us, or we form new creative ideas. Or we realize that there's more to life than sitting on the couch with a pint of Ben & Jerry's, feeling like the victim. Instead, we find ourselves willing to take control of our lives by flowing with it instead of against it.

What's Your Story, Morning Glory?

If you could write yourself an EPIC story of your life, what would you include? Who would be in it? What sorts of milestones would you include? Pretend your life is a book for a second (a best seller, even) and you are the author. (You can write this down if you want.) When you read a book, you want it to capture your attention so you keep reading, right? No one's going to read a book about how you get up and feed the dog every single day unless you make it an EPIC story. Answer these questions for yourself:

1. **What are the EPIC turning points you've already experienced in your life?** These can be experiences of emotional turmoil or complete bliss; either works.

2. **What are the twisted story lines you've experienced from your past?** We all have them, but we forget just how many twists and turns our lives take over the course of a lifetime.

Now, create your EPIC future. Bullet point the rest of your story (or do it in your head; I don't care). This might sound crazy, but let's use your imagination a little bit here. If you were to create an EPIC storyline for the rest of your life from this point on, what would it entail? What would you like to happen next in your life? (It's okay if it seems impossible now).

SO, now that you've done that, no story is complete without a totally EPIC ending.

3. **If you were to add the perfect ending to your life story, the ending of all endings, the one that makes you want to read your next three books because you felt so touched by it, what would that look like for you?** Remember, make sure it's of EPIC proportion. Anything less is unacceptable for this exercise.

The key here is to not make you feel stupid; it's to get you out of your logical thinking and think BIG. Forget all the old beliefs going through your mind and instead focus on what your life would look like if you surpassed your own limitations.

The Journey is the Destination

So once you've found your purpose, then what? Is that the end point? Are you enlightened at that point? Realize that your journey IS your destination. There isn't an end point. "Well, Jen, isn't death technically the end?" Honestly, it depends on what you believe. I don't believe that death is our end point. Sure, our physical body dies, but there's no denying that energy cannot be destroyed. Where does it go? That's for us to find out. So many people fear death and dying, but if you look at it from the perspective that it's actually freeing you from a three-dimensional dense world and allowing you things you always thought were impossible, then maybe you wouldn't view it as such a bad thing after all.

We don't really know what comes next or if we'll be given another go at life, so that's why this is your great opportunity to make the most of it now. It's time to fulfill your destiny and live as that highest amazing version of you, to feel aligned and in the flow of your life, to live with dignity and bliss and to wake up every single day like it's the best damn day of your life. That is my hope for you, but it's up to you. You always have the choice.

Conclusion

It's my hope that you found the information in this book useful and insightful in some way. Maybe you learned something new, maybe you didn't, but all I know is that you are on the path to a huge shift. By changing your mindset and things that have been holding you back, you now realize that your reality is nothing more than a reflection of your internal state. At the end of the day, you can decide which reality you prefer to live in: one from your past where you're always searching for answers, or a reality where you already have all you need. It's a matter of tapping in, getting to know yourself again, and coming back to home base. Many of us have felt lost at one time or another, have struggled with pain, disease, or addiction. But when you make the decision that this isn't you anymore and step into a new version of you, it's the biggest decision you'll ever make in your life.

So in summary, let's reiterate those twelve steps and let them sink in. Revisit these whenever you feel the need for a helping hand, and just know that you're always being guided by your higher self. Remember: you are innately powerful beyond belief.

Step 1: Recognize your ego. Say hello to it.
After all, it's protected you for your entire life and still tries to keep you in your safe place. You might as well get to know it better.

Step 2: We're all made of the same stuff.
Energy. Atoms. Space juice. We're all in this together.

Step 3: Discover WHY you think the way you do.
We are the sum of our own beliefs. We view certain things as real because we were taught or trained to from our past experiences.

Step 4: Recognize that you have the power to choose your reality.
YOU rule your life. Not the other way around.

Step 5: Make the conscious choice to align with your Ideal Reality.
Recognize that you hold the power in your own hands.

Step 6: Embrace your uniqueness. Give up attachments.
Be different by being you. Ain't no one like you on this planet.

Step 7: Realize that it's never selfish to want what you REALLY want.
What's selfish (and foolish) is pretending to want what others want.

Step 8: Release your grip, detach, and go find your inner cheerleader.
She's there waving her pom-poms at you. I promise.

Step 9: Connect with others from a heart space, not a head space.

The heart IS the connection between all things. It's constantly leading and loving you.

Step 10: Believe it before you see it. Don't wait to believe it after you see it. That never works.

Step 11: Discover the power of inner work. Nourish your inner child. It's like feeding your child-self a cherry lollipop and giving your soul a big hug. The more you show love and embrace the both of them, the happier they'll be.

Step 12: Add value to others. You always have a message to share, whether you know it or not. You always have the ability to influence others with your badass self.

Recommended Reading

Dispenza, Joe, *Breaking the Habit of Being Yourself* (Carlsbad, CA: Hay House, 2012).

Dodson, Frederick. *Parallel Universes of Self* (Self Published, 2016).

Franckh, Pierre, *The DNA Field and the Law of Resonance* (Rochester, VT: Destiny Books, 2009).

Hicks, Esther and Jerry, *Ask and It Is Given* (Carlsbad, CA: Hay House, 2004).

Macioca, Giovanni, *The Foundations of Chinese Medicine* (New York, NY: Churchill Livingston Inc., 1989).

McDonagh, Barry, *DARE: The New Way to End Anxiety and Stop Panic Attacks* (BMD Publishing LTD, 2015).

Murphy, Joseph, *The Power of Your Subconscious Mind* (New York, NY: Penguin Group, 1963).

Nelson-Isaacs, Sky, *Living in Flow: The Science of Synchronicity and How Your Choices Shape Your World* (Berkeley, CA: North Atlantic Books, 2019).

Peirce, Penney, *Frequency: The Power of Personal Vibration* (Hillsboro, OR: Beyond Words Publishing, Inc., 2009).

Simmons, Robert, *The Book of Stones, Revised Edition: Who They Are and What They Teach* (Berkeley, CA: North Atlantic Books, 2015).

Surprise, Kirby, *Synchronicity: The Art of Coincidence, Choice, and Unlocking Your Mind* (Newbury port, MA: New Page Books, 2012).

Talbot, Michael, *The Holographic Universe* (New York, NY: Harper Collins Publishers, 1991).

Tolle, Eckhard, *The Power of Now* (Novato, CA: New World Library, 1999).

Zeland, Vadim, *Reality Transurfing: Steps I-V* (St Petersburg, RU: Ves Publishing Group, 2012).

Zeland, Vadim, *Tufti the Priestess* (St Petersburg, RU: Ves Publishing Group, 2012).